GHETTO SERENITY

NAVIGATING LIFE'S HOOD SHIPS
WITH FAITH AND FORTITUDE

By: Dr. Sasha Johnson

DEDICATION

To my amazing sons, Nicholas and Ryan,

This book is for you, my guiding lights and the reason behind every word. Nicholas, your endless curiosity and deep wisdom inspire me to grow and learn every day. Ryan, your boundless energy and infectious laughter remind me to find joy and wonder in each moment.

You both have taught me so much about love, resilience, and strength. Your unwavering belief in me has been my rock through life's ups and downs. This book captures the lessons I've learned and the dreams I hold for your futures.

May you always know how deeply I love you and find guidance in the stories and wisdom within these pages as you walk your own paths. Trust in God, cherish your unique journeys, and never forget that you have the power to achieve greatness.

With all my love, Mom

Table of Contents

INTRODUCTION

I am sure if we realized how important it is to keep a divine connection when it comes to having relationships—which we will describe as "hood ships" in this book—we would understand that we have the ability to choose better for ourselves. Welcome to "Ghetto Serenity: Navigating Life's Hood Ships with Faith and Fortitude." This book is a journey through the complexities of life in the hood, a place where relationships are tested, loyalties are questioned, and challenges are ever-present. It's about finding peace and strength amidst the chaos, using faith as our guiding light through the darkest of times.

We all have our battles with the hood ships of life. These are the relationships that shape us, challenge us, and sometimes break us. In the hood, a solid relationship is built on mutual support, honesty, trust, and respect. It's about standing by each other through thick and thin, ensuring that both parties stay winning and happy. But as we all know, life doesn't always go according to plan. Betrayals happen, trust is broken, and alliances are strained.

The inspiration for this book comes from my own experiences navigating these hood ships. I've been through the highs and lows, the victories and defeats, and everything in between. I've loved hard, lost big, and learned even bigger. Through it all, I've come to realize that the

"

only way to truly navigate these turbulent waters is by anchoring myself in faith and fortitude.

Faith has been my guiding light, much like the scripture from Psalm 119:105 says, "Your word is a lamp for my feet, a light on my path." This verse emphasizes the importance of seeking guidance from God's word as we navigate life's journeys. It reminds us to rely on the wisdom found in Scripture to illuminate our path and guide our decisions, much like a ship relies on a lighthouse to navigate safely.

In this book, we'll explore various aspects of navigating life's hood ships, starting with the importance of keeping it 100 with yourself. We'll delve into personal stories and reflections, like the time I found myself lost in the hustle and bustle of downtown Atlanta because I wasn't paying attention to the guidance right in front of me. These experiences taught me the value of trusting in God's direction and the dangers of trying to forge my own path without His light.

We'll also discuss the significance of faith as your ride-or-die. Just like in the movie *Teen Wolf*, where the main character has to embrace his true self and harness his unique abilities, we too must embrace our faith and use it to guide us through the challenges we face. Faith isn't just a passive belief; it's an active force that propels us forward, giving us the courage to live authentically and pursue our true desires.

Throughout this book, we'll touch on the importance of community and support. Just as a GPS system provides updates on road conditions, a faith community offers support, encouragement, and wisdom.

Surrounding ourselves with a supportive community helps us see dangers we might miss on our own and offers alternative routes when the path ahead seems impassable.

"Ghetto Serenity: Navigating Life's Hood Ships with Faith and Fortitude" is about finding peace in the midst of chaos, strength in the face of adversity, and clarity in times of confusion. It's about trusting that God has a plan for us, even when the road ahead is unclear. It's about using our faith as an anchor to hold us steady, guiding us through the complexities of life with confidence and grace.

So, as you read through these pages, I invite you to reflect on your own journey. Consider the hood ships you've navigated, the potholes you've swerved past, and the lessons you've learned along the way. Let this book be a source of encouragement and inspiration, reminding you that with faith and fortitude, you can navigate any storm and find your way to serenity.

Welcome to the journey. Let's navigate these hood ships together, with faith as our compass and fortitude as our strength.

CHAPTER 1

"Navigating Life's Waters: Introduction to Hood Ships"

Scripture: Proverbs 3:6

"In all your ways acknowledge Him, And He shall direct your paths."

This verse emphasizes acknowledging God in all aspects of life, including navigating life's hood ships. It suggests that by seeking God's guidance, one can confidently and assuredly navigate through life's challenges.

Allow me to begin by acknowledging that if you're someone who has grappled with finding clarity in your journey through relationships and has encountered challenges in maintaining consistent connections, you may find yourself feeling somewhat frustrated with the insights presented in this book. The truth is everyone has battle with the hood ships of life and I know you're probably wondering what I mean by hood ships. In the hood, a solid relationship is when you have each other's backs, keep it real in your talks, trust one another, and show mad respect. It's about working together through the ups and downs, holding each other down, and making sure you both stay winning and happy. But we all know this is not how the story always goes for those type of relationships.

In my experience, I've come to realize that some of the strongest connections I've had weren't the ones society would typically endorse. Take, for instance, those ride-or-die folks who had my back; they weren't the ones you'd label as squeaky clean. Some folks judge others based on appearances – like if they don't rock designer gear or boast fancy degrees. But truth is, that stuff don't mean squat when it comes to real bonds and loyalty.

I've delved deep into relationship stuff, observing what's happening in the news and on social media. And what I've noticed is that some folks just don't know how to keep it real. It brings to mind this track by Rocko called "Snakes." He tells the story of two best friends from way back, who had each other's backs for years. You know how it goes in those puppy love days, where nobody bats an eye if your friend dates your old flame. But in Rocko's tale, one friend ends up with the other's ex, seeking revenge for some childhood slight.

It's sad, but real talk, these hood relationships can go left real quick. In this journey through life's choppy waters, we're diving deep into the world of hood ships. It's a terrain where loyalty is tested, trust is earned, and alliances are forged in the crucible of the streets. From childhood friends turned foes to ride-or-die partnerships that defy societal norms, we're exploring the raw, unfiltered reality of relationships in the hood. So buckle up and get ready for a ride as we navigate the highs and lows of these uncharted waters in "Navigating Life's Waters: Introduction to Hood Ships." In the biblical narrative, we find resonance with the wisdom of Proverbs 3:6, which emphasizes the importance of acknowledging a higher power in all our endeavors. Just as the scripture advises us to trust in divine guidance to navigate life's paths, so too do we recognize the significance of staying grounded in our values and principles amidst the complexities of hood ships. Much like the steadfast faith advocated in Proverbs, where acknowledging God leads to direction and clarity, in the hood, acknowledging our moral compass and staying true to our principles can serve as our guiding light through the turbulent seas of loyalty and betrayal.

Anyone who has experienced betrayal knows it cuts deep, leaving you swimming in regret and self-doubt. It can make you question your worth, even paint yourself as the villain, but let me remind you of this truth: it's not about your inadequacy or failure. These moments are God's way of calling you back to Him, steering you towards the divine path He has laid out for you. We have to get real with ourselves— sometimes, we let our "hood ships" overshadow the most crucial relationship of all, the one we have with God. Let's recalibrate our focus, acknowledging Him in every step, and trust that He will guide us through the storm.

"Beloved, it's time to shift our perspective. When betrayal hits, it's not the end of your story—it's a divine invitation to rise higher. God is calling you to reevaluate and realign your connections. Instead of dwelling on the pain, lean into His presence. Seek His wisdom and let Him heal those wounds.

Remember, God's got a plan far greater than any setback or disappointment. He's pruning away what doesn't serve your purpose, preparing you for something greater. Trust in His process. Stay anchored in your faith, and watch how He transforms your pain into power and your trials into triumphs. You are stronger than you think, and with God, you are unstoppable. Keep pressing forward, knowing that every step you take in faith brings you closer to the destiny He has prepared for you."

Just like Chris Gardner in *The Pursuit of Happyness*, there will be moments when you feel like you're at rock bottom, when the betrayals and setbacks seem insurmountable. In the film, Chris faces tremendous adversity and betrayal. Despite losing his home, his wife leaving him, and experiencing numerous setbacks, Chris remains determined to provide a better life for his son.

In a particularly powerful moment, Chris and his son are forced to spend the night in a subway bathroom. As Chris struggles to hold back his tears, he keeps his son close, protecting him from the harsh reality of their situation. This moment is a testament to his resilience and faith. Despite the overwhelming odds, Chris refuses to give up.

Chris didn't let his circumstances define him; he kept his faith and continued to press forward. He trusted in a greater plan, just as we must trust in God's plan for us. In the end, Chris's persistence paid off, transforming his pain into a powerful testimony of triumph.

Navigating life's waters, especially in the hood, often involves facing tough situations and navigating complex relationships, or "hood ships." Like Chris, you may encounter betrayals and challenges that seem overwhelming. But remember, with God guiding your steps, you are unstoppable. Every challenge you face is shaping you for the destiny God has prepared for you. Keep pressing forward, knowing that your faith and resilience will help you navigate these waters and reach the purpose God has set for you.

Betrayal and Self-Reflection

When I think about betrayal and self-reflection, I often think about the internet and how it seems to go out at the slightest hint of a stronger wind. How often do we jump to self-sabotage, immediately questioning ourselves and our actions? "Lord, did I forget to pay the bill? Is that why my connection is down?" Instead of pausing to consider that maybe, just maybe, it's not our fault at all.

These moments of introspection require us to dig deeper, to peel back the layers and uncover the truths that lie beneath our immediate reactions. It's in these times of reflection that we must confront the lies we tell ourselves, the false narratives that say we are to blame for every disruption, every betrayal, and every hardship.

Self-reflection in these moments is crucial. It's easy to fall into the trap of self-blame, but true self-reflection asks us to go beyond surface-level guilt and examine the deeper issues at play. It requires us to ask, "Why am I so quick to assume the worst about myself?" and "What deeper insecurities are these situations revealing?" By facing these questions head-on, we can begin to heal and grow, rather than getting stuck in a cycle of self-sabotage.

But what if, instead of defaulting to self-blame, we embraced a different perspective? What if we chose to see these interruptions as opportunities for growth and divine redirection? Just as the winds that knock out the internet signal a change in the weather, the storms of life can signal a shift in our spiritual journey, a call to dig deeper and trust in God's plan even when we can't see the way forward.

In the hood, relationships are often tested by these very storms. Loyalty is questioned, trust is broken, and alliances are strained. Yet, it is precisely in these moments of turmoil that we find our true strength. It's when everything seems to fall apart that we discover the resilience that lies within us, guided by a higher power.

When betrayal hits, it's not the end of your story—it's a divine invitation to rise higher. It's a call to reevaluate and realign your connections, to seek God's wisdom and let Him heal those wounds. Remember, God's plan is far greater than any setback or disappointment. He's pruning away what doesn't serve your purpose, preparing you for something greater. Trust in His process. Stay anchored in your faith and watch how He transforms your pain into power and your trials into triumphs. You are stronger than you think, and with God, you are unstoppable. Keep pressing forward, knowing that every step you take in faith brings you closer to the destiny He has prepared for you.

So, the next time the winds blow hard, and your internet goes out, don't rush to blame yourself. Instead, take a moment for self-reflection. Consider the bigger picture and trust that God is with you in every storm, guiding you toward a brighter, more resilient future. Embrace the divine redirection, and let it lead you to the destiny He has lovingly crafted for you.

Do you recall those childhood days, engaged in the spirited game of tug-of-war? Picture it: your team rallying together, each member pulling with all their might, united in the pursuit of victory. Reflecting on this game, I draw a parallel to the intricate dynamics of hood ships. When our team falters, when victory slips through our grasp, it leaves us grappling with feelings of defeat and betrayal. This, my friend, sparks a profound journey of self-reflection, particularly for those of us who possess a competitive spirit like myself.

In the game of tug-of-war, success hinges upon the combined efforts of every participant. Each tug, each exertion of strength, contributes to the collective momentum propelling the team forward. Similarly, in the realm of relationships, the steadfast loyalty, unwavering trust, and steadfast support of every individual are vital to fortifying the bond.

In the hood, where loyalty reigns supreme, the repercussions of betrayal cut deep. Trust, meticulously cultivated, can be shattered in an instant, unleashing a tidal wave of devastation. Hence, the importance of discernment in selecting our comrades, aligning ourselves with souls who mirror our values and stand as unwavering pillars of support.

Yet, even amidst the turmoil of betrayal, there exists a glimmer of hope. Just as a resilient team can regroup and surge forward after a setback in tug-of-war, so too can relationships rebound from betrayal. With time, dedication, and a generous dose of forgiveness, wounds can heal, and bonds can emerge stronger than ever before.

Therefore, when confronted with the sting of betrayal, remember the essence of tug-of-war. Place your trust in the collective strength of your team, for within that unity lies the power to overcome even the most formidable obstacles. With steadfast faith and a supportive community by your side, you possess the resilience to navigate life's turbulent waters and emerge victorious, regardless of the challenges that may come your way.

Reconnecting with Divine Guidance

Let's roll up our sleeves and delve deep into our connection with God. To truly grasp the purpose behind the trials encountered in navigating hood ships, we must strip away the layers and confront the rawness of our reality. I've found myself on bended knee, pleading with God for discernment—to guide me toward cultivating authentic hood ships while steering clear of the repetitive cycles that plague our relational journeys.

As we dissect the intricacies of our experiences, we're called to embrace the power of discernment. Think of it as embarking on the yellow brick road of self-discovery, where each step forward brings us closer to unlocking the divine wisdom woven into the fabric of our lives.

In this pursuit of discernment, we're tasked with peeling back the facade of superficiality, uncovering the genuine connections that lie beneath the surface. It's about recognizing the difference between fleeting alliances and enduring bonds, discerning between those who walk beside us in the light and those who fade into the shadows when darkness descends.

Through prayer, meditation, and introspection, we can hone our ability to discern God's hand at work in our relationships. It's about learning to recognize the subtle nudges of the Holy Spirit, guiding us toward those who uplift and inspire us on our journey.

So, let us embark on this journey of discernment with courage and conviction, trusting that God will illuminate our path and lead us toward the authentic hood ships that align with His divine purpose for our lives.

Wouldn't it be a blessing to receive a warning before the painful revelation of a disloyal friend? Oh, how I've yearned for the gift of foresight, to glimpse the outcome of my relationships before investing my heart and soul. Yet, as I journey through life's complexities, I've come to realize that sometimes, the signs of betrayal are subtle, masked beneath layers of deceit and false promises.

There have been moments when I've felt the unsettling tug of intuition, a whisper of doubt creeping into my spirit. Yet, I've brushed it aside, reluctant to confront the truth lurking beneath the surface. It's in these moments of denial that we forfeit our power of discernment, choosing to turn a blind eye to the warning signs that beckon us to tread carefully.

I'll be the first to admit, there have been times when I've chosen to ignore my instincts, clinging to the hope that things will miraculously improve if I just give it one more chance. But as the old quote goes, "Insanity is doing the same thing over and over again and expecting different results."

It's a sobering truth—one that reminds us of the importance of tapping into our inner wisdom, of acknowledging the red flags that flutter in the wind, signaling danger ahead. For when we refuse to heed the warnings, we risk falling into the same patterns of disappointment and heartache, trapped in a cycle of dysfunction that threatens to engulf us entirely.

So let us embrace our power of discernment, my dear friends, and let us not shy away from the uncomfortable truths that lie in wait. For it is through the lens of discernment that we gain clarity, navigating the murky waters of relationships with wisdom and grace. And though the path may be fraught with uncertainty, we can take solace in the knowledge that with each step forward, we grow stronger, wiser, and more attuned to the whispers of our soul.

Truth be told, we often embark on our journey trusting others, extending the hand of friendship with open hearts and open minds. But as we traverse the landscape of relationships, we soon discover the need for caution, for tuning our ears to the gentle whispers of wisdom bestowed upon us by the Divine.

Yet, in the hustle and bustle of life, it's all too easy to drown out those whispers, to turn a deaf ear to the nudges of intuition that seek to guide us on our path. How often have we found ourselves ignoring the signs, brushing aside the red flags that flutter in the wind, only to be blindsided by betrayal and disappointment?

Here are ten ways to recognize when we're ignoring the power of discernment provided by God:

1. **Ignoring Gut Feelings:** When we dismiss those uneasy feelings in the pit of our stomach, opting instead to forge ahead without pause or reflection.

2. **Rationalizing Behavior:** When we find ourselves making excuses for the questionable actions of others, refusing to acknowledge the truth staring us in the face.

3. **Seeking External Validation:** When we rely on the opinions of others to validate our relationships, rather than trusting our own instincts and intuition.

4. **Ignoring Patterns:** When we fail to recognize recurring patterns of behavior in ourselves or others, repeating the same mistakes time and time again.

5. **Making Excuses:** When we justify staying in toxic relationships or situations, convincing ourselves that things will improve if we just give it more time or effort.

6. **Ignoring Warning Signs:** When we disregard the warning signs that present themselves along our path, choosing instead to plow ahead with blind optimism.

7. **Suppressing Emotions:** When we bury our feelings of doubt, fear, or discomfort, refusing to acknowledge the validity of our emotions.

8. **Ignoring Inner Guidance:** When we neglect to listen to the still, small voice within, dismissing it as mere coincidence or imagination.

9. **Prioritizing Convenience:** When we prioritize convenience or familiarity over our own well-being, settling for relationships that no longer serve us.

10. **Ignoring Counsel:** When we disregard the advice or counsel of trusted friends or mentors, choosing instead to follow our own flawed judgment.

In recognizing these signs, we can begin to reclaim our power of discernment, opening our hearts and minds to the divine guidance that surrounds us. For it is in embracing this gift from God that we find clarity, wisdom, and ultimately, the strength to navigate life's winding paths with grace and resilience.

Realigning Priorities: God Above All

In our quest to reconnect with divine guidance and realign our priorities, we are reminded of a profound story from the Bible—a tale that encapsulates the essence of putting God above all else. It's the story of Mary and Martha, found in the Gospel of Luke.

Mary and Martha were sisters, dear friends of Jesus. On one occasion, Jesus came to visit their home, and Martha was consumed with the preparations, bustling about, ensuring everything was perfect for their honored guest. Meanwhile, Mary sat at Jesus' feet, hanging onto His every word, basking in His presence.

As Martha grew increasingly agitated by her sister's apparent neglect of the household duties, she approached Jesus, asking Him to intervene and instruct Mary to help her. But Jesus gently rebuked her, saying, "Martha, Martha, you are worried and upset about many things, but few things are needed—or indeed only one. Mary has chosen what is better, and it will not be taken away from her."

In this simple yet profound exchange, Jesus conveys a powerful message about priorities. While Martha was preoccupied with the tasks of hospitality, Mary recognized the significance of prioritizing time with Jesus above all else. She understood that the greatest honor she could offer was to sit at His feet, to listen, to learn, and to commune with the divine.

Likewise, in our own lives, we are often inundated with a multitude of responsibilities and distractions, each vying for our attention and energy. Yet, amidst the chaos, it's imperative that we pause, take a step back, and realign our priorities. For ultimately, there is only one thing that truly matters—our relationship with God.

In the hustle and bustle of daily life, it's easy to lose sight of this fundamental truth. We become like Martha, consumed by the demands of the world, neglecting the one thing that can sustain us—the nourishment of our souls through communion with the divine.

But like Mary, we have the opportunity to choose what is better—to prioritize God above all else, to seek His guidance, His wisdom, and His presence in every aspect of our lives. It's a conscious decision to shift our focus from the temporal to the eternal, from the fleeting distractions of this world to the enduring peace found in God's embrace.

So let us take a lesson from Mary's example, dear friends, and let us make the choice to sit at the feet of Jesus, to cultivate a deep and abiding relationship with Him. For in doing so, we will find that all other priorities fall into their rightful place, and we will discover a peace that surpasses all understanding—a peace that can only come from prioritizing God above all else.

As we glean wisdom from the timeless story of Mary and Martha, we are reminded of the paramount importance of realigning ourselves with God. This divine realignment serves as our compass, guiding us through the turbulent waters of life—whether we're navigating hood ships, tapping into the power of discernment, or using pain as a catalyst to draw closer to God.

It's a call to stop conforming to the chaos of this world, to cease allowing the clutter of life to overshadow the clarity of our relationship with the Divine. Instead, we are beckoned to recreate our connection with God, to carve out sacred space amidst the noise and distractions, knowing that in His presence, we find protection, provision, and profound alignment with beneficial hood ships.

Just as Mary chose to prioritize sitting at the feet of Jesus over the flurry of Martha's hospitality, so too must we choose to prioritize our relationship with God above all else. It's in this sacred communion that we discover the strength to navigate the complexities of life with grace and resilience.

As we lean into this divine realignment, we are assured that God will not only protect us but also orchestrate divine connections—hood ships that uplift, empower, and align with His purpose for our lives. These relationships, rooted in the fertile soil of God's love, become sources of strength, support, and solidarity as we journey through life's highs and lows.

So let us heed the wisdom of Mary and Martha, my beloved friends, and let us choose to realign ourselves with God, knowing that in His presence, we find everything we need to navigate the storms of life and emerge victorious on the other side.

In our journey through life's trials and tribulations, it's crucial to remember that pain was never part of God's original design for us. Yet, in the midst of our struggles, we find ourselves grappling with the reality of pain's presence. However, it is precisely in these moments of adversity that we must lean into God's guidance to navigate through the darkness and emerge into the light.

Embedded deep within the core of our being lies an inherent power—a divine spark that ignites our souls and fuels our journey. With God's strength coursing through our veins, our hood ships take on a new dimension, flowing in ways beyond our wildest imagination.

There have been moments in my own journey where the weight of pain threatened to engulf me, where the challenges seemed insurmountable, and giving up felt like the only option. Yet, in those dark hours, I clung to faith like a lifeline, knowing that God's promises endure even in the midst of the storm.

It's in these moments of despair that we are called to dig deep, to tap into the reservoirs of strength that lie dormant within us. For it is through our faith, our resilience, and our unwavering trust in God that we find the courage to press on, even when the path ahead seems shrouded in uncertainty.

Scripture reassures us in Psalm 46:1, "God is our refuge and strength, an ever-present help in trouble." These words remind us that no matter how fierce the storm may rage, God is our shelter, our fortress, and our source of unwavering strength.

So, my dear friend, take heart and hold fast to your faith. For with God by your side, there is no obstacle too great, no challenge too daunting. As you navigate the turbulent waters of life, remember the words of Isaiah 41:10, "Fear not, for I am with you; be not dismayed, for I am your God; I will strengthen you, I will help you, I will uphold you with my righteous right hand."

God's strength is your strength, His wisdom your guide, and His love your anchor in the storm. So keep the faith, dear one, and watch as God transforms your pain into purpose, your trials into triumphs, and your hood ships into vessels of divine grace and blessing.

Let us also recall the journey of Joseph, whose life was marked by betrayal, adversity, and suffering. Despite facing countless trials, Joseph remained steadfast in his faith, trusting in God's plan even when it seemed unfathomable. In Genesis 50:20, Joseph reflects on his experiences, declaring, "As for you, you meant evil against me, but God meant it for good, to bring it about that many people should be kept alive, as they are today."

Joseph's story serves as a poignant reminder that even in our darkest moments, God is at work behind the scenes, weaving together the threads of our lives into a beautiful tapestry of redemption and restoration. Just as Joseph's suffering ultimately led to the preservation of his family and the fulfillment of God's divine purpose, so too can our pain be transformed into a catalyst for growth, resilience, and profound spiritual awakening.

Amidst the challenges of navigating relationships, I've personally encountered seasons where the love I poured out was not reciprocated, where the bonds I cherished seemed to falter under the weight of misunderstanding and betrayal. It's during these times that I've had to confront the harsh reality that not everyone desires our well-being as earnestly as we desire theirs.

Indeed, there are instances when people may unintentionally hurt us, blinded by their own struggles and shortcomings. Yet, there also comes a moment when we must acknowledge that the season of certain hood ships has run its course—a topic worthy of exploration in a future chapter, no doubt.

So, my dear friend, as you navigate the complexities of relationships and the storms of life, may you find solace in the unwavering love of God. May His presence be your guiding light, illuminating your path and empowering you to weather every trial with grace, resilience, and unwavering faith.

SOMETHING HAS TO GIVE

"Navigating Life's Waters: Introduction to Hood Ships" delves into the complexities of relationships, particularly within the context of the hood, where loyalty and betrayal often intertwine. Rooted in Proverbs 3:6, the chapter emphasizes the importance of acknowledging God's guidance in navigating life's challenges, including hood ships.

The chapter begins by defining "hood ships" as relationships characterized by mutual support, authenticity, and respect, often defying societal norms. It highlights the struggles of maintaining genuine connections amidst societal judgments and superficial expectations. Through personal anecdotes and reflections on popular culture, the chapter explores the realities of loyalty and betrayal in hood relationships.

Key themes include:

1. **Betrayal and Self-Reflection:** The chapter delves into the impact of betrayal on self-perception and the importance of introspection in overcoming challenges. It encourages readers to reframe moments of betrayal as opportunities for growth and divine redirection.

2. **Reconnecting with Divine Guidance:** Through prayer and discernment, the chapter urges readers to seek God's wisdom in navigating relationships and discerning authentic connections. It emphasizes the significance of aligning oneself with God's plan amidst life's complexities.

3. **Realigning Priorities**: God Above All: Drawing inspiration from the biblical story of Mary and Martha, the chapter underscores the importance of prioritizing one's relationship with God above all else. It encourages readers to cultivate a deep connection with the divine, finding strength and clarity amidst life's trials.

Questions for reflection:

1. How do you typically respond to moments of betrayal or disappointment in your relationships?

2. In what ways can you deepen your connection with God to navigate life's challenges more effectively?

3. Are there any relationships in your life that may require reevaluation or realignment with God's guidance?

Let us pray: "Heavenly Father, as we navigate the complexities of relationships and the challenges of life, we seek Your divine guidance and wisdom. Help us to discern authentic connections, to prioritize our relationship with You above all else, and to find strength in Your presence. May Your love illuminate our path and guide us through every storm we face. In Your name, we pray, Amen."

CHAPTER 2

"Anchored in Faith: Embracing Hood Ships"

Scripture: Hebrews 6:19 (NIV)
"We have this hope as an anchor for the soul, firm and secure. It enters the inner sanctuary behind the curtain."

This verse speaks to faith being an anchor for the soul, providing stability and security amidst life's storms and challenges. It reinforces the idea of being anchored in faith while navigating various hood ships.

Have you ever felt like a string that is dangling all over the place, without any security or direction? For most of my life, I have felt like the line on a fishing pole with the hook on the end, just floating around, hoping to serve my purpose by finding anchorship in a fish's mouth. I yearned for stability and purpose, but it always seemed just out of reach. I thought simply planting myself would be the answer, but that would only leave me feeling stuck, requiring me to reset my fishing line over and over again.

Many of us find ourselves in a similar predicament. We feel like a fishing line cast out into the vast unknown, without a clear direction or purpose. We hope to latch onto something that gives us meaning, yet we often end up feeling adrift and unanchored. The idea of being plunged into the ground might seem like a solution, but it often leaves us feeling even more stuck, forcing us to continually reset and search for that elusive sense of security and purpose.

Half of you are in need of resetting your line on your fishing pole because you feel stuck, struggling with the loss of firm security and the difficulty of embracing or finding your purpose. It's easy to feel lost when the storms of life toss you around, making it hard to find a stable place to anchor your soul.

But what if the answer lies not in the ground but in the depth of your faith? Hebrews 6:19 reminds us that hope in faith can act as a steadfast anchor for our souls. This anchor doesn't bind us to the ground but secures us firmly, even amidst the tempests of life. It enters the inner sanctuary, providing us with a deeper connection and a sense of peace that transcends the turbulence around us.

Embracing faith means finding that anchor within, one that holds us steady and secure. It allows us to navigate our "hood ships" with a sense of purpose and direction. Instead of resetting our line repeatedly, we can trust in the firm and secure hope that anchors our soul, guiding us through every challenge and storm we encounter.

So, take a moment to reflect. Are you ready to reset your line? To find that firm security and purpose you've been longing for? Anchor yourself in faith, and let it guide you through the waters of life, providing stability and direction. Embrace your "hood ships" with confidence, knowing that your soul is anchored in the hope and faith that lies within.

Imagine being in the hood, where everyone around you seems content with their environment and circumstances. They appear to have accepted their place and are at peace with it. But you, you are different. You constantly go against the grain, always searching for something more. You never feel completely satisfied, yet you pretend this is the right direction for you because you've lost faith in the possibility of any other options beyond your current situation. Can you imagine being the odd one out, the one who feels disconnected and restless?

You can conform and pretend to fit in for as long as you want, but eventually, you'll start to feel powerless. This sense of powerlessness is something your crew will pick up on. They'll sense the disconnect between who you are pretending to be and who you really are. This incongruity can create a perception that you're not being true to yourself, leading them to think you're fake.

The weight of this pretense can be suffocating. Every day, you wake up with a gnawing sense that there has to be more to life than just going through the motions. You see the potential for something greater, but the fear of stepping out and the comfort of the familiar keeps you tethered to your current situation. This internal struggle can be exhausting, leaving you feeling more isolated and misunderstood.

Imagine the freedom that comes from breaking away from this facade. Picture yourself no longer bound by the expectations of others, but instead guided by a deep sense of purpose and authenticity. This isn't an easy journey, but it starts with recognizing the power of faith as your anchor. Hebrews 6:19 tells us, "We have this hope as an anchor for the soul, firm and secure." This hope in faith is what can keep you grounded even when everything around you feels unstable.

By embracing faith, you are not just conforming to the norms of those around you; you are aligning yourself with a higher purpose. Faith provides the clarity and strength needed to navigate the tumultuous waters of life. It allows you to step into your true self, to be authentic in your actions and decisions. When you are anchored in faith, you can withstand the pressures and expectations of the environment around you, finding peace and direction in the midst of chaos.

Imagine the impact of living authentically, guided by faith. Your crew, initially confused by your change, may start to see the strength in your conviction. They might begin to respect the authenticity and courage it takes to live true to oneself. Over time, your genuine actions and steadfast faith could inspire others to explore their own paths and purposes.

This transformation starts with a decision. Decide to reset your line. Decide to anchor yourself in faith. The journey won't be easy, and there will be moments of doubt and difficulty. But with each step, you'll find yourself growing stronger, more resilient, and more aligned with your true purpose. You'll move from a place of pretending and powerlessness to a place of authenticity and strength.

As you embark on this journey, remember that you are not alone. Faith is your anchor, providing the stability and security you need. Embrace your "hood ships" with confidence, knowing that your soul is anchored in the hope and faith that lies within. Let your faith be the anchor that holds you steady, guiding you through life's storms and challenges. Find comfort in the knowledge that by living authentically and anchored in faith, you are on the path to discovering your true purpose and fulfillment.

To help you embark on this journey of authenticity and faith, it's important to start with a practical exercise that grounds you in your intentions and helps you reconnect with your inner truth. This exercise will guide you through a process of self-reflection and commitment, anchoring you firmly in your faith and purpose.

Exercise: The Anchored Reflection

1. **Find a Quiet Space:** Begin by finding a quiet place where you won't be disturbed. This could be a corner of your home, a spot in nature, or anywhere you feel at peace. Bring a journal and a pen with you.

2. **Center Yourself:** Take a few deep breaths to center yourself. Close your eyes and focus on your breathing. As you inhale, imagine drawing in peace and clarity. As you exhale, release any tension or anxiety.

3. **Reflect on Your Current Situation:**

   - Open your journal and write down the ways in which you feel you are conforming to the expectations of others.

   - Describe moments when you have felt disconnected or restless, pretending to be someone you're not.

   - Acknowledge any feelings of powerlessness and the impact this has had on your sense of self.

4. **Identify Your True Desires:**

   - Reflect on what truly makes you feel alive and fulfilled. Write down your passions, dreams, and the values that are most important to you.

   - Consider what steps you would take if fear and doubt were not holding you back. What would you do differently?

5. **Reconnect with Your Faith:**

   - Write down Hebrews 6:19 in your journal: "We have this hope as an anchor for the soul, firm and secure."

   - Reflect on what this verse means to you personally. How can faith act as an anchor in your life, providing stability and direction?

- Write a prayer or affirmation that expresses your commitment to living authentically, guided by faith. Here's an example: "Lord, help me to anchor my soul in Your unwavering love and guidance. Give me the courage to live authentically and to pursue the purpose You have set for me."

6. **Set Intentional Goals:**

- Based on your reflections, set three specific, actionable goals that align with your true desires and values. These goals should move you closer to living an authentic life anchored in faith.

- For each goal, write down a few steps you can take to achieve it. Break these steps into manageable actions you can incorporate into your daily life.

7. **Commit to Regular Check-Ins:**

- Schedule regular times to revisit your journal and reflect on your progress. Use these moments to reassess your goals, celebrate your successes, and adjust your plans as needed.

- Continue to pray and seek guidance, reaffirming your commitment to living authentically and anchored in faith.

Next Steps

By completing this exercise, you are taking the first steps toward breaking free from conformity and embracing your true self. This journey requires continuous effort and dedication, but with each step, you'll find yourself growing stronger and more aligned with your purpose.

Remember, living authentically and anchoring yourself in faith is a transformative process. It may be challenging at times, but the rewards of living a life true to yourself and guided by divine purpose are immeasurable. You will experience a deeper sense of fulfillment, peace, and resilience.

Phew, how does it feel just thinking about the freedom that comes with being faithful and embracing your true self? I don't know about you, but I sometimes struggle with the idea of embracing everything God has laid out for me. There are moments when it feels like God gives me a firm nudge—or even a good spanking—back into alignment. The truth is, this embrace is necessary, or we will ultimately lose ourselves.

You probably didn't expect this chapter on hood ships to turn into a heart-to-heart about getting your life together. But the truth is, I'm not sorry. I want you to reconnect with the power of faith that God has given you. We are all like superheroes in our own right, but sometimes we need to learn how to harness and use our powers effectively, much like the teenage boy in the movie *Teen Wolf.* He had to learn to embrace his true self and the unique abilities that came with it.

In *Teen Wolf,* Scott McCall discovers that he is a werewolf, a revelation that turns his life upside down. At first, he struggles to accept this new identity, fearing the changes and the unknown. However, as he begins to embrace his true self, he learns to control his powers and uses them to navigate the challenges in his life. This journey of self-discovery and acceptance mirrors our own struggles with faith and identity.

Just like Scott, we often grapple with our true identities and the unique purposes God has instilled in us. Initially, it might be overwhelming and even frightening to step into the fullness of who we are meant to be. But through faith, we can find the strength and courage to embrace our true selves. This process of acceptance allows us to harness our God-given powers and navigate life's challenges with greater confidence and clarity.

The key is to remember that embracing our true selves is not a one-time event but an ongoing journey. We will face setbacks and moments of doubt, but it's through these experiences that we grow stronger in our faith and more aligned with our purpose. Embracing faith and our true identity provides a sense of freedom and empowerment that is essential for navigating the complexities of life.

So, as you reflect on this chapter and the exercise, consider the journey of Scott McCall in *Teen Wolf.* Recognize that you, too, have unique strengths and abilities that can only be fully realized through faith and self-acceptance. By embracing your true self and anchoring yourself in faith, you open the door to a life of purpose, fulfillment, and unshakeable confidence.

Let's continue this journey together, leaning on our faith and each other as we navigate the hood ships of life. Embrace the freedom that comes with being faithful and true to yourself. Remember, God has equipped you with everything you need to succeed. All you have to do is trust in Him, embrace your identity, and step boldly into the life He has planned for you.

Keeping It 100 with Yourself

I remember when I was a young single mother trying to find my way. I used to lie to myself so much about what I would accept and what I was okay with in my life. I used to be attracted to guys who seemed street smart, the ones who looked like rough necks. I convinced myself that this was all I deserved—that as long as he had potential, it didn't matter if he didn't have a job. Looking back now, I can't help but laugh at the lies I told myself. It's almost comical, but also frustrating, to think about how I wasn't keeping it 100 with myself. Why do we lie to ourselves so easily, convincing ourselves that what we truly desire is something we can never attain?

The truth is, we often settle for less because we lack faith in our worth and the belief that we deserve better. We convince ourselves to accept less than we desire because it feels safer than reaching for something more. It's easier to stay in a comfort zone, even if that zone is far from what we truly want or need. This mindset keeps us stuck in cycles of dissatisfaction and unfulfillment.

Breaking free from this pattern starts with being brutally honest with ourselves—keeping it 100. It's about acknowledging our true desires and recognizing that we are worthy of them. We have to stop settling for potential and start demanding the real thing. This honesty extends to every area of our lives, including our relationships, careers, and personal growth.

For me, this realization was a game-changer. I had to confront the lies I was telling myself and make a conscious decision to pursue what I genuinely wanted. It wasn't easy, and it required a lot of self-reflection and faith. I had to trust that God had a plan for me that was far greater than the limited vision I had for myself. Hebrews 6:19 became my anchor, reminding me that my hope and faith are firm and secure, providing the stability I needed to move forward.

Once I started keeping it 100 with myself, everything began to change. I no longer settled for less than I deserved. I started setting higher standards for myself and my relationships. I began to see the potential within myself rather than relying on the potential of others. This shift in mindset allowed me to attract better opportunities and healthier relationships, aligning my life more closely with God's purpose for me.

If you're struggling with this, I encourage you to take a step back and reflect on the lies you might be telling yourself. Are you settling for less than you deserve because it's comfortable or familiar? Are you afraid to reach for more because you don't believe you're worthy of it? Keeping it 100 with yourself means addressing these questions head-on and making a commitment to pursue your true desires.

Faith as Your Ride-or-Die

When I look back on my journey, I realize that faith has been my ride-or-die. It's the constant force that has carried me through the ups and downs, the challenges and triumphs. Hebrews 6:19 tells us, "We have this hope as an anchor for the soul, firm and secure." This hope, rooted in faith, is what keeps us grounded and provides the stability we need to navigate life's storms.

Faith isn't just a passive belief; it's an active force that propels us forward. It gives us the courage to be honest with ourselves and to pursue our true desires. It reassures us that we are worthy of more than just potential—we are worthy of greatness. Faith reminds us that God's plans for us are far greater than anything we can imagine.

Having faith as your ride-or-die means trusting that God is guiding you, even when the path isn't clear. It's about leaning into that faith during moments of doubt and using it as a source of strength. When you anchor yourself in faith, you become resilient, able to withstand the challenges that come your way.

So, let's commit to keeping it 100 with ourselves and embracing faith as our ride-or-die. Let's trust that we are worthy of our true desires and that with faith, we can achieve them. By being honest with ourselves and anchored in faith, we can navigate life's hood ships with confidence and grace, knowing that we are on the path to fulfilling our God-given potential.

SOMETHING HAS TO GIVE

Anchor

Question for Reflection:

- Are you anchored in your faith, providing stability and direction in your life, or do you feel adrift and unsteady amidst life's challenges?

Keeping It 100

Question for Reflection:

- What lies have you been telling yourself about your worth and what you deserve? How can you start being brutally honest with yourself about your true desires?

Faith as Your Ride-or-Die

Question for Reflection:

- How can you strengthen your faith to be your guiding force, helping you navigate life's ups and downs with confidence and resilience?

Let us Pray: Heavenly Father, we come before You with open hearts, seeking Your guidance and strength. Help us to anchor ourselves in our faith, finding stability and direction amidst life's storms. Give us the courage to keep it 100 with ourselves, to be honest about our true desires and to pursue them with unwavering faith. Strengthen our faith, Lord, so that it becomes our ride-or-die, guiding us through every challenge and triumph. May we always remember that we are worthy of the greatness You have planned for us. In Your holy name, we pray. Amen.

CHAPTER 3

"Charting Your Course: Reflections on Hood Ships"

Scripture: Psalm 119:105 (NIV)

"Your word is a lamp for my feet, a light on my path."

This verse highlights seeking guidance from God's word as we navigate life's journeys. It emphasizes relying on the wisdom found in Scripture to illuminate our path and guide our decisions, much like a ship relies on a lighthouse to navigate safely.

I remember driving in downtown Atlanta one day and having such a horrible experience. If you know anything about Atlanta, you know about the traffic and the long distances you have to travel just to get to a simple destination. But on this particular day, I decided to get bold and make a turn in the middle of downtown on a road I wasn't familiar with. Knowing me, I had the navigation on but probably wasn't listening to the guidance. Y'all, I say all this to explain that before I knew it, I saw cars coming at me head-on in each lane. When I tell you I freaked out and called on the Lord for help, it was because I realized I should have listened to the guidance from the beginning. I quickly took a turn down a side street, and God saved me. My heart was beating through my chest, but if this isn't a lesson on why we should allow God to navigate our lives, then I don't know what is.

Reflecting on this experience, I realize how often we try to navigate life on our own terms, ignoring the guidance available to us. It's like having a GPS but choosing to take our own route, thinking we know better. Just as I found myself in a dangerous situation by not listening to my navigation, we too can find ourselves in precarious positions when we ignore God's word and rely solely on our judgment.

In our daily lives, it's easy to get caught up in the hustle and bustle, making quick decisions without pausing to seek divine direction. Psalm 119:105 reminds us that God's word is meant to be a guiding light, illuminating our path and helping us make wise decisions. When we neglect this guidance, we risk veering off course and encountering unnecessary difficulties.

Think about your own journey. How often do you forge ahead without consulting the ultimate navigator—God? We might think we have everything under control, but without His guidance, we are bound to encounter obstacles that could have been avoided. Trusting in God's word and allowing it to guide us can save us from a lot of heartache and trouble.

Navigating life's hood ships—those complex and sometimes treacherous relationships and situations—requires more than just our understanding. It requires a steadfast reliance on the wisdom and direction that only God can provide. When we make decisions based on His word, we are like ships steering by the light of a lighthouse, safely navigating through the darkness and avoiding hidden dangers.

Y'all, let's commit to letting God's word be the lamp to our feet and the light on our path. Let's seek His guidance in all areas of our lives, trusting that He knows the best route for us. By doing so, we can navigate the challenges of life with confidence, knowing that we are on the right course, guided by His unwavering light.

Take a moment to reflect on your own life. Are there areas where you need to invite God's guidance more fully? Are there decisions you've been making on your own that you need to submit to His wisdom? As we chart our course, let's make a conscious effort to rely on the divine navigation that God offers, ensuring that we stay on the path He has illuminated for us.

In the coming sections, we'll explore practical ways to incorporate God's guidance into our daily lives and discuss how to recognize when we're straying off course. We'll also share testimonies of how following God's direction has led to breakthroughs and blessings. Together, we can learn to navigate our hood ships with the confidence and assurance that comes from walking in the light of God's word.

Navigating the Concrete Jungle

Driving through the hustle and bustle of downtown Atlanta is a lot like navigating the challenges of everyday life. The traffic, the unexpected turns, and the chaotic energy of the city mirror the struggles we face as we journey through our own concrete jungles. It's easy to get caught up in the madness, thinking we can handle everything on our own. But just like that day in Atlanta, without guidance, we can quickly find ourselves heading straight into danger.

Hey you, it's in these moments that we need to remember that we aren't meant to do this alone. God's word is our map, our navigation system, guiding us through the dense urban sprawl of life's challenges. When we rely on His wisdom, we can avoid the pitfalls and dead ends that lead to frustration and despair. We can trust that even when we can't see the way forward, His light will shine brightly, illuminating our path and showing us the way to safety and peace.

As we navigate our daily lives, it's important to recognize when we are trying to take control and steer ourselves. Often, we hold onto the wheel so tightly, thinking that if we just try harder or plan better, we can avoid the inevitable bumps in the road. But this approach often leads to more stress and confusion. It's like driving in downtown Atlanta without a GPS—you might get somewhere, but it won't be the best or safest route.

This brings to mind the powerful song "Let Go" by DeWayne Woods. The lyrics of this song speak directly to the struggles we face when we try to handle everything on our own. Woods sings about the peace that comes from letting go and letting God take control. "As soon as I stop worrying, worrying how the story ends, I let go and I let God, let God have His way," he sings. These words remind us that our attempts to control every aspect of our journey often lead us to unnecessary stress and anxiety. By letting go and trusting God, we find the freedom and peace that we've been searching for.

"Let Go" encourages us to release our burdens and allow God to lead us. It's a beautiful reminder that we don't have to navigate life's challenges on our own. When we let go and let God, we allow His wisdom and guidance to direct our paths. This act of surrender doesn't mean we give up our responsibilities; rather, it means we trust that God's plan is greater than our own and that He will provide the direction we need.

Imagine how different our lives could be if we adopted this mindset. Instead of clinging to our limited understanding and control, we could embrace the assurance that comes from faith. We could face each day with confidence, knowing that God's word is a lamp for our feet and a light on our path. His guidance is always available to us, illuminating our way even in the darkest of times.

In your own concrete jungle, there will be moments when the path ahead seems unclear and the obstacles insurmountable. It's in these moments that you need to pause, take a deep breath, and let go. Trust that God's navigation system is far superior to any route you could plan on your own. Lean into His word, and let it guide you through the chaos.

By embracing this approach, we allow ourselves to experience the true peace and clarity that come from living a faith-driven life. We begin to see challenges not as insurmountable obstacles but as opportunities for growth and trust in God's plan. Just as a ship relies on a lighthouse to safely navigate through treacherous waters, we too must rely on God's word to guide us through the complexities of life.

So, the next time you find yourself overwhelmed by the hustle and bustle, remember to let go and let God. Allow His word to be the lamp that lights your path and the map that guides your journey. Trust in His wisdom, and you'll find that even in the midst of the concrete jungle, you can navigate with peace, purpose, and confidence.

Listening to Your Inner GPS

Have you ever ignored your GPS, convinced you knew a better route, only to end up lost or stuck in traffic? It's the same with our spiritual journey. We have an inner GPS—God's guidance—that we sometimes ignore because we think we know better. But ignoring this divine direction can lead us into situations we could have easily avoided.

Listening to your inner GPS means tuning into the wisdom of God's word and the nudges from the Holy Spirit. It means being still and allowing yourself to hear the quiet whispers of guidance that God is always offering. When we make a habit of consulting this inner GPS, we become more attuned to the path God has set for us. We start making decisions that align with His plan, and we find ourselves on a smoother, more purposeful journey.

Swerving Past Life's Potholes

Life is full of potholes—unexpected challenges and obstacles that can throw us off course if we're not careful. Just like driving, if we're not paying attention, we can hit a pothole that causes significant damage. But with God's guidance, we can swerve past these obstacles and keep moving forward.

Think of God's word as the ultimate pothole detector. When we're anchored in scripture and prayer, we're better equipped to see the challenges ahead and navigate around them. We can anticipate the bumps in the road and adjust our course accordingly. By staying connected to God and trusting His direction, we can avoid the pitfalls that trip us up and keep our journey as smooth as possible.

When you find yourself disconnected from God, it's like that moment when you realize that Facebook is down, and you find yourself confused and lost. Connecting with your inner self and your faith is your direct connection to God, giving you the clarity and strength to navigate life's challenges. This connection provides you with the insight needed to see the potholes before you hit them and the wisdom to navigate around them.

Navigating hood ships—those intricate, often complicated relationships in our lives—requires the same vigilance and connection to God's guidance. Hood ships can be fraught with their own unique set of potholes: trust issues, loyalty tests, misunderstandings, and even betrayals. Just as we need to be prepared for the unexpected bumps on the road, we need to be spiritually and emotionally prepared to handle the complexities of these relationships.

It's essential to maintain this spiritual connection daily. Just as you wouldn't drive without checking your mirrors or using your navigation system, you shouldn't go through life without checking in with God and using His word as your guide. This practice can involve regular prayer, meditation, and reading scripture. Each of these actions helps you stay tuned in to God's will and prepared for whatever comes your way.

Reflecting on the importance of this connection brings to mind another analogy. Think of your relationship with God like maintaining your car. Regular check-ups and maintenance keep your vehicle running smoothly and help you avoid breakdowns. Similarly, regular spiritual check-ins and maintenance keep your soul running smoothly, helping you avoid emotional and spiritual breakdowns.

When you encounter a pothole in life—a sudden loss, a betrayal, an unexpected challenge—how you handle it depends on your preparation. If you are spiritually prepared, you can swerve around it or absorb the shock without significant damage. Without that preparation, you might find yourself stuck or sidelined, struggling to get back on track.

In the realm of hood ships, this preparation means being grounded in your values and faith. It means knowing when to set boundaries, when to forgive, and when to walk away. By staying connected to God, you gain the discernment needed to navigate these relationships wisely, ensuring they contribute positively to your life rather than detract from it.

Moreover, surrounding yourself with a supportive community can also help you navigate life's potholes. Just as a GPS system provides updates on road conditions, a faith community offers support, encouragement, and wisdom. They can help you see dangers you might miss on your own and offer alternative routes when the path ahead seems impassable.

Remember, the goal isn't to have a journey free of obstacles—because that's not realistic. The goal is to be so grounded in faith that when those obstacles appear, you're ready. You're able to navigate them with grace and confidence, knowing that you're guided by a higher power.

As you continue to chart your course through life and navigate your hood ships, keep this metaphor in mind. Stay vigilant, stay connected, and stay anchored in faith. With God's word as your ultimate pothole detector, you can confidently swerve past life's challenges and keep moving toward your divine destination.

Reflect on your own life. Are there areas where you've hit a pothole and struggled to recover? How can you use your faith to better anticipate and navigate these challenges? By integrating these practices into your daily routine, you'll be better equipped to handle whatever comes your way, ensuring a smoother journey filled with purpose and peace.

SOMETHING HAS TO GIVE

Navigating the concrete jungle of life requires us to stay connected to our inner GPS and be vigilant about swerving past life's potholes. As we chart our course, let's commit to relying on the light of God's word to guide us. Let's seek His wisdom in every decision and trust that He will lead us safely through the chaos and confusion.

Question for Reflection:

- Are you actively seeking God's guidance in your daily life, or are you trying to navigate on your own terms?

Prayer: Heavenly Father, thank You for being the light that guides our path. Help us to navigate the complexities of life with Your wisdom and grace. Teach us to listen to our inner GPS and trust Your direction, even when the road ahead is unclear. Strengthen our faith so that we can swerve past the potholes and obstacles that come our way. May we always rely on Your word as our anchor, providing stability and security in every situation. In Jesus' name, we pray. Amen.

CHAPTER 4

"Surviving the Streets: Faith and Fortitude "

Scripture: Proverbs 16:9

"In their hearts humans plan their course, but the Lord establishes their steps. "

This verse speaks to reflecting on life's journeys and the hood ships we navigate, highlighting the importance of trusting in God's guidance and sovereignty even as we make plans and decisions.

You might find this strange or look at me with the side eye when I tell you that I don't think I would consider where I was raised to be the hood, but maybe some do. My brother and I often have different perceptions of our upbringing. He sometimes refers to our neighborhood as the hood, while I see it differently. This difference in perception made me realize that our experiences are subjective, and neither of us is necessarily wrong.

We grew up in Montgomery, Alabama, a place I've nicknamed "Little Memphis" due to the increasing crime rate there now. When I say I have no desire to move back, I mean it wholeheartedly. But it makes me question: was there a lot of crime back then that I chose to ignore? Did I survive by masking and ignoring possible truths?

I remember staying on the Northside of town, which is a little rough now. Truth be told, we were only a few miles from what was considered the projects or the real hood. We lived in a predominantly black community, and there were a lot of odd things happening. If I remember correctly, one of our neighbors was on the local news for shooting himself in the foot, which seems funny to me now.

As I tell this story, I think about survival. Survival is often defined as continuing to live or exist despite hardship or adversity. But do we sometimes survive by ignoring the truth? If what we perceive isn't the full reality, are we truly surviving? This thought left me in shambles. Have I survived, or am I still in this battle with myself?

Navigating the streets of life can be as treacherous as it is exhilarating. In the hood, every day presents new challenges and opportunities, testing our resilience and faith. We may plan our paths with the best intentions, but it's crucial to remember that it is the Lord who ultimately establishes our steps. This chapter is about recognizing God's guiding hand in our lives and finding the strength to persevere through the toughest of times with faith and fortitude.

Growing up in the hood, I've seen firsthand how important it is to hold onto faith. There were times when the streets felt like an endless maze of uncertainty and danger. It was easy to get lost, to feel overwhelmed by the challenges that came my way. But even in the darkest moments, I found solace in knowing that God was with me, guiding my steps and providing the strength I needed to keep going.

Metaphorically, we all have to survive our own hoods. If you think of the hood as a symbol for life's challenges and strains, then we all have our own "hoods" to navigate. Life can throw us into difficult situations where we feel lost, overwhelmed, and in danger. These hoods are where our resilience and faith are truly tested. And that seems hood enough to me.

When we talk about surviving the streets, we're talking about more than just getting by. We're talking about thriving amidst adversity, finding hope in hopeless situations, and relying on our faith to see us through. It's about understanding that our plans might not always align with God's plans, but trusting that His path for us is always the best one.

One of the most significant bullet wounds in my life was witnessing my biological parents fight and eventually divorce. Even though I have since gained two amazing bonus parents, the confusion and emotional turmoil caused by their breakup profoundly impacted the way I viewed marriage. By all means, this was not my parents' fault. It was my perception and the lens through which I chose to see things. I remember the anger and sadness I internalized, seeing their pain through my child's eyes. It left me confused and hurt, but now, as a mature adult, I realize it was one of God's steps in guiding me, using my parents as vessels.

One of the most valuable lessons I've learned is that resilience isn't just about bouncing back from setbacks; it's about growing stronger through them. Each challenge we face is an opportunity to deepen our faith and fortify our spirits. When we encounter obstacles, we can either let them break us or use them as stepping stones to elevate our lives.

In the hood, relationships—or hood ships—are crucial to our survival and success. These connections can either uplift us or drag us down, depending on how we navigate them. Proverbs 16:9 reminds us that while we may plan our course, it is God who establishes our steps. This means that even in our relationships, we must seek divine guidance to ensure we are aligning ourselves with people who support and encourage our growth.

Surviving the streets also means being adaptable and resourceful. It's about learning to make the most out of limited resources and finding creative solutions to the problems we face. This adaptability is rooted in a deep trust in God's provision and a willingness to follow His lead, even when the path is unclear.

Reflecting on my own journey, I remember times when I had to rely solely on faith to get through. There were moments when I had no idea how I would make it to the next day, but God always provided a way. He placed the right people in my life, opened doors I never expected, and gave me the strength to keep pushing forward.

One powerful example of resilience and faith in action is the story of Joseph in the Bible. Sold into slavery by his brothers, falsely accused and imprisoned, Joseph faced immense hardship. Yet, through it all, he remained faithful to God. His resilience and trust in God's plan ultimately led him to a position of great power and influence, where he was able to save many lives, including those of his own family.

Joseph's story is a testament to the fact that no matter how dire our circumstances may seem, God is always at work behind the scenes, guiding our steps and preparing us for a greater purpose. It's a reminder that surviving the streets isn't just about enduring; it's about thriving and becoming a beacon of hope and strength for others.

As you reflect on your own journey, consider how God has guided your steps, even when the path was difficult. Think about the ways in which your faith has sustained you and given you the fortitude to keep going. Remember that every challenge is an opportunity to grow stronger and deepen your trust in God.

Bullet Wounds: Scars of Survival

In the hood, metaphorical and sometimes literal bullet wounds are part of the landscape. These wounds—be they physical, emotional, or spiritual—tell stories of the battles we've faced and the resilience we've shown. Each scar, whether visible or hidden, is a testament to our survival and our journey through adversity.

Bullet wounds can come in many forms. They might be the loss of a loved one, a betrayal by someone you trusted, or the constant struggle against systemic obstacles that seem designed to hold you back. These wounds hurt, and they leave marks, but they also shape who we are and how we navigate the world.

The key to dealing with these wounds is not just to survive but to heal and grow stronger. Healing requires us to confront the pain, to acknowledge our scars, and to seek out the support and resources that can help us move forward. Faith plays a crucial role in this healing process. By turning to God, we find the strength to face our wounds, the wisdom to learn from them, and the courage to keep moving forward.

In your own life, consider the bullet wounds you've endured. How have they shaped you? What lessons have they taught you? Reflect on how your faith has helped you heal and grow stronger. Remember, every wound is an opportunity to deepen your resilience and fortitude, and to find new ways to navigate life's challenges with grace and wisdom.

Divine Detours: Trusting the Unexpected Path

Life often takes us on unexpected journeys. These divine detours can be disorienting and challenging, but they are also opportunities for growth and transformation. When our carefully laid plans are disrupted, it's easy to feel frustrated and lost. However, these moments are when we must trust in God's greater plan for our lives.

Jeremiah 29:11 says, "For I know the plans I have for you," declares the Lord, "plans to prosper you and not to harm you, plans to give you hope and a future." This verse reassures us that even when we are faced with unexpected detours, we can trust that God is guiding us toward a greater purpose. These divine detours are not setbacks but redirections, leading us to places we might never have reached on our own.

Think about the detours in your life. Maybe you didn't get the job you wanted, a relationship ended, or you faced a health crisis. At the moment, these events may have felt like roadblocks, but over time, you may have seen how they led you to new opportunities, relationships, and personal growth that you wouldn't have experienced otherwise.

One of the most significant divine detours in my life was when I found myself lost in the hustle and bustle of downtown Atlanta. Despite having the navigation on, I wasn't listening to the guidance. This experience taught me a valuable lesson about the importance of paying attention to God's direction and trusting His plan, even when it takes us down unexpected paths.

In the Bible, we see countless examples of divine detours. Think of Moses, who fled Egypt and spent 40 years in the desert before leading the Israelites to freedom. Or Ruth, whose journey to a foreign land led her to become the great-grandmother of King David. These stories remind us that God's detours are filled with purpose and potential.

Reflect on the divine detours in your life. How have they shaped your journey? How has your faith helped you navigate these unexpected paths? Embrace these detours with an open heart, trusting that God is leading you toward a greater purpose. By doing so, you can find peace and assurance in the midst of life's uncertainties, knowing that every step you take is guided by His divine wisdom.

Have you ever felt like Dorothy from *The Wizard of Oz*, not knowing the path but also not trusting in yourself, despite being powered by God?

I have experienced this feeling, particularly in friendships and romantic relationships where discernment was screaming that they were not right for me. Now, there's that word—discernment—again. I was trying too hard to communicate what couldn't be explained and to repair what couldn't be repaired. As I think about these situations, it brings me to tears, remembering the frustration I felt in wanting to make those relationships work. The truth is, I was more saddened by the feelings of rejection and failure, which don't feel good.

These divine detours taught me the importance of listening to God's guidance and trusting in His plan. Instead of forcing relationships or situations to work out, I learned to let go and let God direct my path. This not only spared me from unnecessary heartache but also opened doors to new, more fulfilling relationships and opportunities.

God's plans for us are always rooted in love and purpose. By trusting Him through every twist and turn, we can find the strength and courage to face life's uncertainties. Remember, every detour is a chance to grow in faith, build resilience, and discover the incredible plans God has for your life.

Reflect on your own divine detours. How have they redirected your life in ways you couldn't have imagined? How has your faith been strengthened through these unexpected paths? Embrace the journey with an open heart, knowing that God's wisdom and love are guiding you every step of the way.

SOMETHING Has to Give

Navigating the streets of life requires resilience, faith, and the willingness to embrace both the wounds and detours that come our way. By trusting in God's guidance, we can turn our scars into sources of strength and our unexpected paths into opportunities for growth. As you reflect on your journey, remember that God is with you every step of the way, providing the faith and fortitude you need to thrive.

Question for Reflection:

- How has God guided your steps through the challenges you've faced in life, and how has your faith helped you navigate these obstacles?

Prayer: Heavenly Father, thank You for being our constant guide and source of strength. Help us to trust in Your plans for us, even when the path is difficult and uncertain. Give us the resilience and fortitude to navigate the streets of life with faith and courage. May we always seek Your guidance in our decisions and relationships, knowing that You are with us every step of the way. In Jesus' name, we pray. Amen.

CHAPTER 5

"Voyage of Discovery:
Embracing Hood Life"

Scripture: Proverbs 3:5-6 (NIV) -

"Trust in the Lord with all your heart and lean not on your own understanding; in all your ways submit to him, and he will make your paths straight."

This scripture speaks to embracing life's journeys and hood ships with trust in God's guidance, even when the path seems uncertain. It encourages reliance on God's wisdom rather than solely on our understanding.

The world of confusion that leaves us with uncertainty and shame often leads us to discovery. We sometimes find ourselves searching for the context clues of life, but maybe we need a different view. Are we embracing the issues of life or merely reacting to the situations when we say that "life be lifing"? Are those challenges our hidden context clues set by God?

I can't help but think back to the kids' show "Blue's Clues" and wonder if we are navigating a show in our own lives like Blue's Clues. I never really liked the show, but maybe it's because I was the actor in my own show, trying to discover myself in my personal hood ship.

Life often presents us with challenges and obstacles that seem confusing and overwhelming. We may feel like we're constantly searching for answers, much like the character in Blue's Clues who looks for clues to solve a puzzle. In the show, the host, with the help of the animated dog Blue, looks for paw prints left by Blue as clues to solve a mystery. Each clue brings the host closer to understanding the bigger picture. Similarly, our life challenges are like those clues, guiding us towards a deeper understanding and growth.

Often, the confusion and chaos we experience in life can feel like we are wandering aimlessly, but what if these moments are actually opportunities for growth? What if the very challenges we face are God's way of guiding us toward a deeper understanding of ourselves and our purpose? Each trial and tribulation can be seen as a clue left by God, directing us toward greater clarity and wisdom. It's in these moments of struggle that we are often closest to the breakthroughs that define our journeys.

Instead of merely reacting to life's situations, we should strive to embrace them, seeing each challenge as a step on the path to discovery. It's easy to feel overwhelmed when things don't go as planned, but by shifting our perspective, we can see these challenges as integral parts of our story. Much like the host of Blue's Clues, we need to be patient and attentive, looking for the hidden messages in our experiences. By doing so, we allow ourselves to grow and learn, becoming more aligned with God's plan for our lives.

Proverbs 3:5-6 tells us to "Trust in the Lord with all your heart and lean not on your own understanding; in all your ways submit to him, and he will make your paths straight." This means that even when we don't understand why certain things are happening, we can trust that God is guiding us. The clues He leaves for us might not make sense immediately, but with faith and patience, their purpose will become clear.

In my own life, there have been countless times when I felt lost and confused, unsure of the path ahead. But looking back, I see how each of those moments was a crucial part of my journey. Each challenge was a clue, guiding me toward greater self-awareness and understanding. Whether it was dealing with difficult relationships, career setbacks, or personal struggles, every experience has contributed to my growth.

What if we viewed every obstacle not as a hindrance but as a clue? How would that change the way we approach life? By embracing this mindset, we can turn even the most challenging situations into opportunities for growth and discovery. We can start to see the beauty in the struggle and the lessons hidden within our toughest battles.

As we navigate our personal hood ships, let's remember that we are not alone. God is with us, providing the clues we need to find our way. By trusting in His guidance and embracing the challenges we face, we can move forward with confidence and faith, knowing that every step brings us closer to our true purpose.

So the next time life feels overwhelming, take a step back and look for the clues. Trust that God has a plan, and every challenge is a part of it. Embrace the journey, and you'll discover the incredible growth and wisdom that come from navigating life's obstacles with faith and perseverance. Let's do some work.

Exercise: Finding God's Clues

Objective: To help you recognize and reflect on the "clues" God is providing in your life, leading you towards growth and understanding.

Materials Needed:

- Journal or notebook
- Pen or pencil
- A quiet space for reflection

Instructions:

1. **Reflect on Past Challenges:**

   - Take a moment to think about some significant challenges or obstacles you've faced in your life. Write them down in your journal. Consider both recent and past events.

2. **Identify the Clues:**

   - For each challenge, try to identify the "clues" or lessons you believe God was providing. Ask yourself:

     - What did I learn from this experience?

- How did this challenge help me grow or change for the better?

- Were there any positive outcomes or new opportunities that arose from this situation?

3. **Connecting the Dots:**

- Look at the clues you've identified. How do they connect to each other? Do you see a pattern or a recurring lesson that God might be trying to teach you? Write down your thoughts and observations.

4. **Future Challenges:**

- Think about any current challenges you are facing. How can you apply the lessons you've learned from past experiences to your current situation? Write down any insights or actions you can take to navigate your current challenges with faith and trust in God's plan.

5. **Prayer and Meditation:**

- Spend a few moments in prayer or meditation, asking God to help you see the clues He is providing in your life. Ask for the wisdom to understand His guidance and the courage to follow His path, even when it seems uncertain.

6. **Regular Reflection:**

- Make it a habit to regularly reflect on the challenges you face and the lessons you learn. Use your journal to document your journey and to remind yourself of God's constant presence and guidance.

Trusting in the Divine Game of Hide and Seek

When I think back to my childhood, one game that comes to mind is hide and seek. We would run around, trying to find the best hiding spots, and the seeker would have to trust their instincts and clues to find us. Much like this game, our journey with God often feels like a divine game of hide and seek. We are searching for Him in the midst of our challenges, trusting that He will reveal Himself and His plans at the right time.

In the Bible, Jeremiah 29:13 says, "You will seek me and find me when you seek me with all your heart." This verse reminds us that God is not hiding to remain unfound; He desires to be discovered and understood. Our role is to actively seek Him with our whole heart, trusting that He will guide us through the clues He provides.

How many of us half-step when seeking God and struggle with the feeling that we need to question everything about Him? I know I have been this person, and honestly, I still battle with this sometimes. When we face challenges, it's easy to feel lost and doubt God's presence in our lives. But just like in hide and seek, we must trust that the clues are there and that God is leading us, even when we can't see Him.

I remember going through significant challenges in my marriage, dealing with self-doubt, infidelity, and physical abuse. These experiences left me feeling rejected, worthless, and like I was being beaten down, both physically and emotionally. It was a dark and confusing time, and I often questioned God's presence and purpose for my life.

But I had to come to a crucial realization: perception. My ex-husband couldn't be anything for me that he had never seen or experienced himself. This understanding didn't excuse his behavior, but it helped me see that his actions were a reflection of his own brokenness, not my worth.

The Puzzle Pieces of Life

Another childhood memory that aligns with our theme is putting together a jigsaw puzzle. Each piece of the puzzle represents different events and challenges in our lives. At first, the pieces may seem random and disconnected, but as we begin to fit them together, a clearer picture emerges.

Romans 8:28 reassures us, "And we know that in all things God works for the good of those who love him, who have been called according to his purpose." Just like a puzzle, every piece of our lives, no matter how confusing or painful, is part of a greater design. Trusting that God is working all things together for our good allows us to find peace and purpose in the midst of life's challenges.

As children, we would often start with the edges and the corners of the puzzle, building the framework first before attempting to fill in the middle. Similarly, in our lives, we sometimes need to establish our foundational beliefs and values to help us make sense of the more complex and intricate parts of our journey. These foundational pieces might include our faith, our relationships, and our sense of purpose.

When we encounter particularly challenging or painful pieces of our puzzle, it can be tempting to set them aside and focus only on the easier parts. However, it's often through grappling with these difficult pieces that we gain the most profound insights and growth. Each piece, no matter how seemingly insignificant or overwhelmingly complex, contributes to the overall picture that God is creating in our lives.

Now let me come back to the current state of reality, which is that I am no longer a child, but looking at discovery from another lens can help us understand ourselves and find the joy of embrace. We are not the only people that have stories of discovery. I used my pain from my previous marriage to allow God to guide me.

Stories of Discovery

1. **Joseph's Journey:**

   - Joseph's story in the Bible is a profound example of trusting God's guidance through life's twists and turns. Betrayed by his brothers, sold into slavery, falsely accused, and imprisoned, Joseph's journey was full of unexpected detours. However, each step was a clue leading to God's greater plan for him to save many lives during a famine. Joseph's faith and trust in God's plan allowed him to rise to a position of great power and fulfill his purpose (Genesis 37-50).

2. Ruth's Loyalty:

- Ruth's loyalty to her mother-in-law Naomi led her to an unexpected path. After losing her husband, Ruth chose to stay with Naomi and return to Bethlehem. Her decision, though challenging, led her to meet Boaz, through whom she became the great-grandmother of King David. Ruth's story is a testament to how divine detours and faithful decisions can lead to blessings beyond our imagination (Ruth 1-4).

3. Paul's Mission:

- The Apostle Paul faced numerous trials, including imprisonment, shipwrecks, and persecution. Despite these challenges, Paul trusted God's guidance and continued his mission to spread the Gospel. His letters, written during times of great adversity, continue to inspire and guide Christians today. Paul's life exemplifies how trusting in God's plan can turn obstacles into opportunities for profound impact (Acts 9-28).

These stories, much like our own, are filled with moments of confusion, uncertainty, and challenge. Yet, by trusting in God's guidance and looking for the clues He provides, we can navigate our personal hood ships with faith and resilience. Each story reminds us that our challenges are not the end but part of a greater journey towards discovering God's purpose for our lives.

In it all, our journey of discovery is much like a divine game of hide and seek, a complex puzzle, and a series of transformative stories. By seeking God wholeheartedly, trusting in His timing, and finding joy in the process, we can navigate the twists and turns of our lives with faith and hope. As we look for the clues God provides, we begin to see the beautiful tapestry He is weaving in our lives, leading us towards our ultimate purpose and destiny.

SOMETHING HAS TO GIVE

As you navigate your own life's journey, consider this: How can you shift your perspective to see the challenges you face as clues from God guiding you towards growth and deeper understanding? What steps can you take to trust more fully in His plan, even when the path seems unclear?

Let us pray: Heavenly Father, we come before You with hearts full of gratitude for Your constant presence and guidance in our lives. We thank You for the lessons and the growth that come from the challenges we face. Help us to seek You with all our hearts and to trust in Your perfect plan, even when we don't understand the path ahead. Give us the patience to see the bigger picture, the courage to embrace each step, and the faith to know that You are weaving all things together for our good. Surround us with a supportive community that encourages us and helps us see Your hand at work in our lives. May we find joy in the journey and peace in Your promises, knowing that every piece of our puzzle is part of Your beautiful design. In Jesus' name, we pray. Amen.

CHAPTER 6

"Journey to the Horizon:
Tales of Hood Ships"

Scripture: Psalm 107:23-30 (NIV)
"23 Some went out on the sea in ships;
they were merchants on the mighty waters.
24 They saw the works of the Lord,
his wonderful deeds in the deep.
25 For he spoke and stirred up a tempest
that lifted high the waves.
26 They mounted up to the heavens and went down to the depths;
in their peril their courage melted away.
27 They reeled and staggered like drunkards;
they were at their wits' end.
28 Then they cried out to the Lord in their trouble,
and he brought them out of their distress.
29 He stilled the storm to a whisper;
the waves of the sea were hushed.
30 They were glad when it grew calm,
and he guided them to their desired haven."

This passage vividly depicts the journey of sailors facing turbulent waters, calling out to the Lord in distress, and being guided safely to their destination. It reflects the ups and downs of life's journey, the challenges faced, and the faith in God's guidance through it all.

When I say the term "turbulent waters," it strikes a deep chord within me. The first thing that comes to mind is the multitude of storms—tsunamis, tornadoes, and hurricanes—that people endure during their hood ships. Many have no idea how much we battle or are still battling to stay grounded. This is where I have to emphasize the importance of minding our own business, especially if we are not willing to walk through the battlefields of those we idolize. Now, that was a whole word.

The tales of hood ships are the narratives we create and assume we understand, when in reality, we are often ignorant of the true struggles. Without God leading us on this journey, where would we be? Each of us has a unique path, and we will never have the same results or experiences as the next person. God promises us His guidance and support through it all.

Navigating the turbulent waters of life often feels like steering a small boat through a massive storm. The waves crash against us, the wind howls, and we struggle to keep our balance. In these moments, it can be tempting to look at others who seem to be sailing smoothly and wonder why our journey is so fraught with difficulty. But we must remember that appearances can be deceiving. Just because someone's ship seems steady doesn't mean they aren't facing their own unseen storms.

It's easy to get caught up in comparing our hood ships to others, thinking that their lives are easier or more blessed than ours. This comparison is not only unfair to ourselves but also overlooks the unique challenges that everyone faces. Each of us has our own journey, and God's plan for us is tailored to our individual needs and growth. What we perceive as smooth sailing for others might just be a different kind of test or lesson that they are meant to learn.

Our hood ships are deeply personal experiences that shape who we are and who we become. The storms we weather, the battles we fight, and the challenges we overcome all contribute to our growth and resilience. It's through these experiences that we develop a deeper understanding of ourselves and a stronger faith in God's guidance. Without these trials, we would not be the people we are today, capable of empathy, strength, and perseverance.

I remember a particularly challenging time in my life when I felt completely overwhelmed by the storm I was facing. It was as if every aspect of my life was being tested, and I couldn't see a way out. During this time, I found solace in Psalm 46:1-3, which says, "God is our refuge and strength, an ever-present help in trouble. Therefore we will not fear, though the earth give way and the mountains fall into the heart of the sea, though its waters roar and foam and the mountains quake with their surging." This passage reminded me that no matter how fierce the storm, God is always with us, providing strength and refuge.

The truth is, we often don't know the full extent of someone else's hood ship. We see only the surface, not the deep waters they are navigating. It's important to approach others with compassion and understanding, recognizing that everyone is fighting their own battles. Instead of judging or comparing, we should offer support and encouragement, helping each other stay afloat in the stormy seas of life.

There have been times when I've felt like giving up, when the weight of the storm seemed too much to bear. In those moments, it's crucial to remember that we are not alone. God is our constant companion, guiding us through the darkest times. His promises are steadfast, and His love is unwavering. When we feel like we can't go on, we can lean on Him for strength and courage.

One of the most powerful examples of enduring turbulent waters with faith is the story of Job. Despite losing everything—his wealth, his family, his health—Job remained steadfast in his faith. He questioned and lamented, but he never turned away from God. In the end, God restored Job's fortunes and blessed him even more abundantly than before. Job's story reminds us that, no matter how severe our trials, God's faithfulness and love will see us through.

Another story that comes to mind is that of David, who faced numerous battles and personal struggles throughout his life. From his encounter with Goliath to his flight from King Saul, David experienced many turbulent waters. Yet, his psalms are filled with expressions of trust and reliance on God. Psalm 23, one of the most well-known and beloved psalms, beautifully captures this trust: "The Lord is my shepherd, I lack nothing. He makes me lie down in green pastures, he leads me beside quiet waters, he refreshes my soul." Even in the midst of chaos, David found peace in God's presence.

Our hood ships are opportunities for us to draw closer to God, to rely on His strength, and to grow in faith. Each storm we face is a chance to deepen our relationship with Him and to trust in His plan for our lives.

It's through these experiences that we learn to let go of our need for control and surrender to His will.

Reflecting on my own journey, I can see how each storm has shaped me and strengthened my faith. The battles I've fought, the challenges I've faced, and the pain I've endured have all contributed to my growth. I've learned that God's timing is perfect, even when it doesn't align with my own plans. He knows what we need and when we need it, and His guidance is always for our ultimate good.

In the midst of our hood ships, it's important to keep our eyes on God and to trust in His promises. Isaiah 43:2 says, "When you pass through the waters, I will be with you; and when you pass through the rivers, they will not sweep over you. When you walk through the fire, you will not be burned; the flames will not set you ablaze." This assurance gives us the courage to face whatever comes our way, knowing that God is with us every step of the journey.

As we navigate our turbulent waters, let us remember that God's guidance is our anchor. He will lead us through the storms, calm the waves, and bring us to our desired haven. Our hood ships are not meant to defeat us but to refine us, to build our character and deepen our faith. With God by our side, we can weather any storm and emerge stronger and more resilient on the other side.

The Flames Will Not Ablaze You

When we think about the storms we face and the fires we walk through, we are reminded of the resilience and strength that comes from trusting in God's guidance. This profound truth is powerfully illustrated in the story of a girl from the show "Gen V," who possesses the unique and challenging power to control blood. Her journey is a poignant reminder that even the fiercest trials will not consume us when we believe in ourselves and trust in a higher power.

In "Gen V," we meet a young girl named Marie, who has the ability to manipulate blood. From a young age, Marie struggled with her powers, often feeling overwhelmed and afraid of the destruction she could cause. One tragic night, her emotions got the best of her, and she accidentally unleashed her powers, resulting in a devastating accident that killed her parents. This traumatic event left Marie with deep guilt and a fear of her own abilities.

Marie's journey is marked by her battle to control her powers and find a place where she belongs. She is sent to a special school for individuals with extraordinary abilities, where she hopes to learn how to harness her blood manipulation and prevent further harm. However, the path is not easy. She faces judgment from her peers, who know about her past, and she struggles with self-doubt and the fear that she is inherently dangerous.

Despite these challenges, Marie begins to find her strength. She learns that her powers, when controlled and understood, can be a force for good. She meets mentors and friends who help her see that her past does not define her and that she has the potential to use her abilities to protect and save others. Through training and self-discovery, Marie gains confidence and starts to embrace who she is.

Marie's story beautifully parallels the message in Isaiah 43:2, which says, "When you pass through the waters, I will be with you; and when you pass through the rivers, they will not sweep over you. When you walk through the fire, you will not be burned; the flames will not set you ablaze." Just as Marie learns to walk through her own literal and figurative trials, we are reminded that God's presence in our lives ensures that we will not be consumed by the challenges we face.

As Marie navigates her journey, she encounters numerous storms, both internal and external. She has to confront her guilt and fear, and she must also deal with the distrust and hostility from those around her. These storms test her resolve and push her to the brink, but they also forge her into a stronger, more resilient individual.

Marie's turning point comes when she realizes that her powers are not a curse but a gift. She learns to channel her blood manipulation with precision and purpose, using it to protect those she cares about and to fight against those who seek to do harm. Her journey teaches her that true strength comes from within, and that by believing in herself and trusting in the guidance of her mentors, she can overcome any obstacle.

This story of resilience and redemption is a powerful reminder that we, too, have the strength to face our storms. The trials that threaten to consume us are the very fires that refine us and reveal our true potential. Like Marie, we must learn to trust in ourselves and in the higher power that guides us through the darkest times.

Marie's journey also highlights the importance of community and support. She finds strength in her relationships with others who understand her struggles and who stand by her side through thick and thin. This mirrors our own need for a supportive community that can help us navigate our hood ships. When we surround ourselves with those who uplift and encourage us, we are better equipped to face the challenges ahead.

The story of Marie from "Gen V" is a testament to the transformative power of faith and self-belief. Despite her tragic past and the immense challenges she faces, she emerges stronger and more determined to use her abilities for good. Her journey is a vivid illustration of the scripture's promise that the flames will not set us ablaze, and that through God's guidance, we can overcome any storm.

As we reflect on Marie's story and the storms in our own lives, let us hold onto the promise that we will not be consumed by the trials we face. Instead, we will be refined and strengthened, emerging from our trials with a deeper understanding of our purpose and a stronger faith in God's plan. With each step we take, let us remember that we are not alone, and that God's presence is a constant source of strength and guidance.

Power In the Rolling Hills

My good people, now I must share this song that you must listen to by Jill Scott called "Rolling Hills." Even though she was speaking directly to women, I felt the message deeply resonate with all people. What if we think of "rolling hills" like turbulent waters and challenges that help us on our journey to our horizons?

Jill Scott's "Rolling Hills" is a powerful anthem about embracing one's true self and finding strength in the face of adversity. She sings about the natural curves and contours of a woman's body, comparing them to the rolling hills of a landscape. But if we take a broader view, these rolling hills can symbolize the ups and downs of life, the peaks and valleys we all navigate on our journey.

Just as hills rise and fall, so do the challenges and triumphs in our lives. Each hill represents a hurdle to overcome or a lesson to learn. Boy, have I learned many lessons. When we face these "hills," we have two choices: we can see them as insurmountable obstacles or as opportunities to grow and strengthen our faith. The latter perspective aligns perfectly with the themes we've been exploring—the idea that God uses our struggles to shape us into the people we are meant to be.

Think about the rolling hills in your own life. What challenges have you faced that seemed impossible at the time but ultimately led to growth and transformation? Perhaps it was a difficult relationship, a career setback, or a personal loss. Each of these hills, though daunting, provided valuable lessons and pushed you closer to your horizon.

Let me break it down with a street hood example. Imagine a young man named Jamal, growing up in a tough neighborhood. Every day, he faces the rolling hills of his environment—gang violence, peer pressure, and limited opportunities. One day, he decides he wants something different for his life. He starts studying hard, avoiding trouble, and dreaming of college. The journey is anything but smooth. He's ridiculed by his peers for not conforming, he's tempted to take shortcuts, and he sometimes feels the weight of his decisions. But Jamal keeps climbing those hills, one step at a time. Eventually, he earns a scholarship and gets accepted into a good university. Each hill he climbed, each challenge he faced, only made him stronger and more determined. Jamal's story shows that by facing our rolling hills with faith and resilience, we can overcome and reach our goals. You too, can climb the rolling hills of your life.

The metaphor of rolling hills also reminds us of the journey we are on. Just as a hiker must keep moving forward to reach the peak, we too must continue pressing on, even when the path is steep and the climb is tough. Philippians 3:14 says, "I press on toward the goal to win the prize for which God has called me heavenward in Christ Jesus." This scripture encourages us to keep our eyes on the prize, knowing that each step, each hill we climb, brings us closer to our divine purpose.

Moreover, the rolling hills can be seen as a landscape crafted by God, full of beauty and purpose. In Psalm 121:1-2, it says, "I lift up my eyes to the mountains—where does my help come from? My help comes from the Lord, the Maker of heaven and earth." These verses remind us that God is the creator of the hills and the valleys, and He is our source of strength as we navigate them.

Embracing the power in the rolling hills means acknowledging that our struggles are not in vain. They are part of the intricate design that God has for our lives. Each challenge we face is a step toward the greater plan

He has for us. By shifting our perspective and seeing the hills as opportunities rather than obstacles, we can harness the power within us to overcome and thrive.

Jill Scott's song also speaks to the importance of self-acceptance and self-love. As we face our rolling hills, we must remember to be kind to ourselves. Recognize that it's okay to struggle and it's okay to stumble. What's important is that we get back up and keep moving forward. Each hill conquered is a testament to our resilience and our faith in God's guidance.

Reflect on your own journey and identify the rolling hills you have faced. How have these challenges shaped you? How have they helped you grow closer to God? Embrace the strength you have gained from these experiences and use it to face future hills with confidence and faith.

In essence, the rolling hills of our lives, much like the turbulent waters we navigate, are integral to our journey. They test our strength, build our character, and draw us closer to God. By embracing the power within these hills, we can continue our journey with a sense of purpose and determination, knowing that every step we take is guided by His loving hand.

SOMETHING HAS TO GIVE

Question for Reflection: How can you embrace the rolling hills in your life as opportunities for growth and deeper faith?

Let us pray: Heavenly Father, we thank You for the rolling hills in our lives that challenge us and help us grow. Help us to see these hills not as obstacles, but as opportunities to strengthen our faith and draw closer to You. Grant us the resilience and courage to keep pressing on, even when the path is steep. Remind us of Your constant presence and guidance, and fill our hearts with the peace that comes from trusting in Your plan. In Jesus' name, we pray. Amen.

CHAPTER 7

"Life's Shipyard: Building Hood Relationships with Purpose"

Scripture: Ecclesiastes 4:9-10

Ecclesiastes 4:9-10 underscores the importance of companionship and mutual support in life. It emphasizes the strength found in unity and cooperation, highlighting the value of meaningful relationships built on trust and shared purpose.

"Two are better than one, because they have a good return for their labor: If either of them falls down, one can help the other up. But pity anyone who falls and has no one to help them up."

Ecclesiastes 4:9-10 underscores the importance of companionship and mutual support in life. It emphasizes the strength found in unity and cooperation, highlighting the value of meaningful relationships built on trust and shared purpose.

Sometimes, I think that we come up with every excuse in the book for why we hold on to certain people. Maybe we hold on because comfort and familiarity feel safer than change. Personally, I was struggling with "people pleasing" as a reason for holding on. I had no real purpose for some of these relationships. I remember asking myself, what am I benefiting from this connection? What is the point of this relationship? I like to think of some hood ships as seasons, and I personally enjoy a "hot girl summer," while some of my friends that I have tried to hold on to are stuck in winter or fall.

In life's shipyard, we are constantly building and rebuilding our relationships. Some relationships are like sturdy ships, capable of weathering any storm. Others are like fragile boats, barely holding together. It's crucial to evaluate the purpose and value of these relationships, ensuring that they contribute positively to our lives and spiritual growth.

Reflecting on my own journey, I realized that some of my hood ships were based on convenience rather than genuine connection. I held onto these relationships out of fear of being alone or discomfort with change. Ecclesiastes 4:9-10 reminds us that true companionship is about mutual support and lifting each other up. If a relationship doesn't serve this purpose, it may be time to let go.

Building hood relationships with purpose means being intentional about the people we surround ourselves with. It's about choosing friends and partners who share our values, support our growth, and encourage us to be our best selves. These are the relationships that stand the test of time and provide a solid foundation for our personal and spiritual development.

Just as a ship needs a strong hull to navigate rough waters, we need strong, purposeful relationships to help us navigate life's challenges.

These relationships act as our support system, providing encouragement, wisdom, and accountability. They help us stay grounded and focused on our goals, even when the seas get rough.

However, it's important to recognize that not all relationships are meant to last forever. Some people come into our lives for a season, serving a specific purpose before moving on. It's okay to let go of relationships that no longer align with our growth and purpose. Holding onto these relationships out of habit or fear can hinder our progress and keep us stuck in the past.

When evaluating our hood ships, we should ask ourselves if these relationships help us grow spiritually, emotionally, and mentally. Do they inspire us to be better? Do they provide support during tough times? If the answer is no, it might be time to reassess and make necessary changes.

One way to build purposeful relationships is by setting clear boundaries and communicating openly with those around us. Let people know what you need and expect from the relationship. This not only fosters trust and respect but also ensures that both parties are on the same page and working towards a common goal.

In addition to boundaries, mutual respect and understanding are key components of strong relationships. Respecting each other's differences, supporting each other's dreams, and being there during challenging times are all essential. Ecclesiastes 4:10 emphasizes the importance of lifting each other up. In a purposeful relationship, when one person falls, the other is there to help them get back up.

Moreover, building hood relationships with purpose means being selective about who we invest our time and energy in. Not everyone deserves a place on our ship. Surround yourself with people who genuinely care about your well-being, who challenge you to grow, and who celebrate your successes as if they were their own.

To put this into practice, start by identifying the key relationships in your life. Reflect on their impact on you. Are they positive and uplifting, or do they drain your energy and pull you down? Be honest with yourself about the nature of these relationships and be willing to make tough decisions if necessary.

Remember, it's not about the quantity of relationships, but the quality. A few meaningful, purposeful relationships can have a far greater impact on your life than many superficial ones. Invest in relationships that matter and let go of those that don't.

Cut Them Off

Like O.T. Genasis said so gracefully in his song, "You need to cut it." By no means am I saying that this is an easy task. When I tell you that I did everything in my power to fix the relationships instead of cutting them off, believe me, it was like taking a burned-out motor out of a car, attempting to fix it with no guidance and no knowledge, and then putting it back in the car only for it to break down on the side of the road again.

One of the main reasons we hold on to these dysfunctional relationships is because we seek approval and try to avoid rejection. Ironically, we should be rejecting those toxic and nonbeneficial relationships instead. When we constantly strive for approval, we end up compromising our own well-being and values.

Individuals who constantly seek to please others often agree to things they don't actually want to do out of fear of rejection and a deep desire for approval. This behavior can result in neglecting their own needs and priorities. The continuous effort to keep others happy can lead to significant stress, frustration, and damage to relationships, as it often results in a lack of genuine interaction and a feeling of being undervalued.

By clinging to these toxic relationships, we are essentially choosing to remain in a state of discomfort and dissatisfaction. It's like repeatedly putting a faulty motor back into the car, hoping that this time it will work, even though we know it's bound to fail. Instead of wasting time and energy on relationships that are not meant to be, we need to have the courage to cut them off and make space for healthier, more fulfilling connections.

Cutting off toxic relationships is not an act of cruelty; it's an act of self-preservation. It's recognizing that your well-being is important and that you deserve relationships that uplift and support you. When you let go of the relationships that drain you, you create room for those that bring joy and growth into your life.

Moreover, maintaining toxic relationships can stunt our personal growth. When we are constantly trying to fix what's broken, we don't have the energy or the space to focus on our own development. It's essential to recognize when a relationship is hindering your progress and take the necessary steps to move forward.

It's also important to understand that not all relationships are meant to last forever. Some people come into our lives to teach us lessons, and once those lessons are learned, it's time to move on. Holding onto these relationships out of a sense of obligation or fear can prevent us from experiencing new opportunities and connections.

When we cut off toxic relationships, we are setting boundaries and reinforcing our self-worth. We are telling ourselves and others that we deserve respect, love, and kindness. This act of self-respect can inspire others to treat us with the same level of consideration and care.

It's natural to feel guilty or uncertain about ending a relationship, especially if we've invested a lot of time and emotion into it. However, it's crucial to remember that your primary responsibility is to yourself and your well-being. By prioritizing your needs, you are better equipped to nurture and sustain the relationships that truly matter.

Letting go of toxic relationships also allows us to break free from negative patterns and behaviors. When we are no longer surrounded by negativity, we can begin to see things more clearly and make decisions that are in our best interest. This clarity can lead to a more fulfilling and purposeful life.

Finally, by cutting off toxic relationships, we empower ourselves to build a life that reflects our true values and desires. We create space for positivity, growth, and genuine connection. We learn to value ourselves and our time, understanding that we deserve relationships that nurture and support us. This newfound strength and clarity can transform our lives, leading us to greater fulfillment and happiness. Take a moment to recite these follow affirmations aloud to yourself.

- *I deserve relationships that honor my values and respect my boundaries.*

- *Setting boundaries is an act of self-care and self-respect.*

- *I have the right to prioritize my well-being and personal growth.*

- *I can say no without feeling guilty or ashamed.*

- *Healthy boundaries lead to more meaningful and fulfilling relationships.*

- *My needs and feelings are valid and important.*

- *Establishing boundaries allows me to connect with others authentically.*

- *I am worthy of relationships that uplift and support me.*

- *Creating space for myself helps me to nurture my own happiness and peace.*

- *I attract positive and respectful relationships by maintaining clear boundaries.*

Forgiving Yourself for Settling

Now, I am about to lay it all out because this chapter is really hitting my spirit. Letting go is one of the hardest things that I have ever had to do. It sometimes literally feels like I am pulling my hair out. One thing that I had to let go of and forgive myself for is the relationship I had with my past self. I would choose to do things or stay in situations because I thought this was what others wanted. I can hear my mom saying now, "You know that is not true." For example, let me go back to my previous marriage. I convinced myself that I didn't have the money for a divorce at the time, but if I'm being honest with y'all, I didn't want to fail at my marriage despite the pain I endured. I didn't want people judging me for being messed up. These were my thoughts. I had to forgive myself for lying to myself and accepting this type of treatment. Honestly, I was almost chasing an ideal that I could fix him and save him when the only person that could save us both was God. I have realized where purpose lacked in this relationship.

Self-forgiveness is a crucial step in moving forward from the mistakes and compromises we've made in the past. It's easy to be hard on ourselves, replaying the decisions that led us to settle in relationships that weren't right for us. But beating ourselves up doesn't change the past; it only hinders our growth. We must learn to extend the same compassion to ourselves that we would to a friend who made similar mistakes.

In my journey, I had to confront the fact that I often prioritized others' expectations over my own needs and desires. This realization was painful, but it was necessary for my healing. Acknowledging that I had settled allowed me to start the process of forgiving myself. I began to understand that my worth wasn't tied to someone else's opinion or approval.

Forgiving yourself means letting go of the guilt and shame associated with past decisions. It means understanding that you did the best you could with the knowledge and resources you had at the time. I had to accept that staying in a painful marriage was a choice I made out of fear and a lack of self-worth. Recognizing this helped me to start rebuilding my self-esteem and making better choices for my future.

One significant aspect of self-forgiveness is recognizing that we are all human and prone to making mistakes. It's part of our journey to learn and grow from these experiences. Holding onto regret only keeps us anchored in the past, preventing us from embracing the possibilities of the future. By forgiving myself, I freed myself from the chains of past mistakes and opened the door to new, healthier relationships.

Another important step in forgiving yourself is to focus on the lessons learned rather than the pain endured. My failed marriage taught me valuable lessons about my own strength, resilience, and the importance of self-love. Instead of viewing the experience as a failure, I began to see it as a crucial part of my growth. This shift in perspective allowed me to move forward with a renewed sense of purpose.

Forgiving yourself also involves acknowledging the role you played in settling but not letting it define you. Yes, I made choices that led to my unhappiness, but those choices don't determine my worth. By taking responsibility without self-condemnation, I was able to reclaim my power and start making decisions that aligned with my true self.

It's important to remember that forgiveness is a process, not a one-time event. There were days when the weight of my past decisions felt unbearable, but each time I chose to forgive myself, the burden lightened. Over time, this practice of self-forgiveness became a cornerstone of my healing journey.

One of the most liberating aspects of self-forgiveness is the realization that you have the power to change your narrative. I stopped seeing myself as a victim of my circumstances and started viewing myself as the author of my own story. This empowerment was key to rebuilding my life with intention and purpose.

In this journey of self-forgiveness, I also learned the importance of seeking God's guidance. Prayer and meditation became essential tools in helping me find peace and clarity. By surrendering my pain and regrets to God, I found the strength to forgive myself and trust in His plan for my life.

As I forgave myself, I noticed a significant change in my relationships. I began attracting people who respected and valued me, reflecting the newfound respect and value I had for myself. This transformation was a testament to the power of self-forgiveness and the importance of building relationships based on mutual respect and purpose.

Ultimately, forgiving yourself for settling is about embracing your past, learning from it, and moving forward with a heart full of compassion for yourself. It's about recognizing your worth and making choices that honor your true self. By doing so, you pave the way for a future filled with healthy, purposeful relationships and a deeper connection to your own divine journey.

Embracing New Beginnings

As we journey through the shipyard of life, building and evaluating our hood ships, it's important to remember that every ending brings a new beginning. Each time we let go of a relationship that no longer serves us, we create space for something new and potentially more fulfilling. This process requires faith and trust in God's plan for us.

Jeremiah 29:11 reminds us, "For I know the plans I have for you," declares the Lord, "plans to prosper you and not to harm you, plans to give you hope and a future." This verse reassures us that God's plans for us are good, even when we can't see the path ahead. Trusting in His guidance allows us to embrace new beginnings with hope and confidence.

Building purposeful relationships also means being open to the unexpected. Sometimes, the most meaningful connections come from places we least expect. By staying open and receptive, we allow God to bring the right people into our lives at the right time. Proverbs 27:17

says, "As iron sharpens iron, so one person sharpens another." Surround yourself with those who challenge you to grow and be your best self.

In the process of building these relationships, it's essential to remember that quality matters more than quantity. It's better to have a few deep, meaningful connections than many superficial ones. These relationships will be the anchor that keeps us grounded during life's storms. Philippians 1:3-4 expresses the value of such connections: "I thank my God every time I remember you. In all my prayers for all of you, I always pray with joy."

Reflecting on your journey, ask yourself: What lessons have I learned from my past relationships? How have these experiences shaped me into the person I am today? Embrace the wisdom gained and use it to build a future filled with relationships that honor God's purpose for your life.

As we close this chapter, remember that building hood relationships with purpose is a continuous process. It requires intentionality, self-reflection, and a willingness to grow. By aligning ourselves with God's plan and surrounding ourselves with supportive, uplifting people, we can navigate life's shipyard with confidence and grace. Each relationship is a step towards fulfilling our divine purpose, and with God's guidance, we can build a life rich with meaningful, purposeful connections.

Let us pray: Heavenly Father, we thank You for the relationships You have placed in our lives. Help us to build and nurture connections that align with Your purpose. Give us the wisdom to let go of relationships that no longer serve us and the courage to embrace new beginnings. Guide us in setting boundaries that honor our worth and allow us to grow. May we find strength and support in the community You provide, and may our relationships reflect Your love and grace. In Jesus' name, we pray. Amen.

CHAPTER 8

"Sailing Through Storms: Lessons from Hood Ships"

Scripture: Isaiah 43:2

Isaiah 43:2 offers comfort and assurance during difficult times, assuring believers that God will be with them through life's trials and challenges. It provides confidence that despite facing storms, God's presence will safeguard them.

One of my clients once asked me, "What do you do after changes have set in and now the purposeful relationships or hood ships that you are currently in are being affected? What do you do?" When I say, I was lost for words and uncertain of what to say. The truth is, I know all about the aftermath of toxic relationships and not understanding the lessons that I am supposed to gain from them. This is when I really have to tap into the power of the Lord, honey. People often think that as a therapist, I am supposed to have it all together, but I absolutely do not. I didn't know the answer, and this truly bothered me.

I guess it is no different than the meteorologist telling us on the news that it is going to storm when there ends up being a sunny day with no rain in sight. So, let's think about this. I remember when I worked a 9-5 and was always the overachiever, for what reason, I have no idea. But either way, I became burned out from the overload of clients, extra hours, and the number of deaths I experienced. I had a co-worker who was killed by her husband, who then killed himself, leaving three children behind. I had a client who killed himself and his mom in a murder-suicide, and the list goes on. This was a career hood ship, and this job had no care about how all this was affecting me emotionally. I had to figure my way out of this storm. What was the lesson for me?

I was choosing everyone but myself, for one. I had to realize the whispers God had been sending me. I had to let that job go with the quickness. The message was there all along that I needed to set better boundaries. The truth is, I had to stop ignoring the truth and settling because I set limitations on what I thought I could accomplish.

One thing that stands out to me about these storms is that they often serve as wake-up calls. They force us to re-evaluate our priorities and make necessary changes. When we're in the midst of the storm, it's hard to see clearly. But once we start to listen to God's whispers and pay attention to the signs, we begin to understand the purpose behind the pain. It's in these moments that we grow the most.

For example, think about how Jesus calmed the storm in Mark 4:39. He rebuked the wind and said to the waves, "Quiet! Be still!" Then the wind died down, and it was completely calm. Jesus asked His disciples, "Why are you so afraid? Do you still have no faith?" This passage reminds us that no matter how fierce the storm, Jesus has the power to bring peace and calm.

Just like in that passage, we must have faith that God is with us in our storms. It's easy to feel abandoned and lost when we're facing hardships, but Isaiah 43:2 reassures us that we will not be consumed by the flames. God is our protector and guide, even when we can't see the way forward.

Another important lesson from these storms is learning to prioritize self-care. We can't give what we don't have. When I was overwhelmed with my job and the trauma it brought, I neglected my own needs. I had to learn to set boundaries and take care of myself first. This was crucial in finding balance and maintaining my mental health.

Self-care isn't just about taking breaks; it's about recognizing our worth and understanding that we deserve to be treated with kindness and respect. It's about making choices that align with our values and well-being. Sometimes, this means making difficult decisions, like leaving a toxic job or ending a harmful relationship.

Moreover, storms teach us the importance of community. We are not meant to weather these challenges alone. Galatians 6:2 emphasizes the value of bearing one another's burdens: "Carry each other's burdens, and in this way, you will fulfill the law of Christ." In times of trouble, having a strong support system can make all the difference. Surround yourself with people who uplift you and provide encouragement.

Reflect on the story of Job. Despite losing everything, Job remained faithful to God. His friends came to comfort him, although they were not perfect in their counsel. Ultimately, Job's faith was restored, and he was blessed with even more than he had before. This story teaches us about perseverance and the importance of relying on God and our community during tough times.

As we sail through the storms of life, let's remember that these experiences shape us. They build our character and strengthen our faith. The key is to remain steadfast and trust that God has a plan, even when it's not clear to us. It's about finding peace in the midst of chaos and knowing that we are never alone.

Take the time to reflect on the lessons you've learned from your own storms. How have they shaped you? What changes have you made as a result? Embrace these experiences as opportunities for growth and transformation. By doing so, you'll find that even the most difficult challenges can lead to greater resilience and wisdom.

Remember, the storms we face are not meant to destroy us but to refine us. They push us to grow, to trust in God more deeply, and to make changes that align with His plan for our lives. Remember Isaiah 43:2 and hold on to the promise that we will not be consumed. With God by our side, we can navigate any storm and come out stronger on the other side. Let's try this activity, below.

Activity: Identifying Lessons from Life's Storms

Understanding the lessons from life's storms can be a transformative process. This activity is designed to help you reflect on your experiences, recognize the lessons they hold, and find ways to apply these lessons to your life. Set aside some quiet time for this activity, grab a journal or a piece of paper, and let's get started.

Step 1: Reflect on Your Storms

Think about a few significant challenges or "storms" you have faced in your life. These could be personal, professional, or relational struggles. Write down each one in detail. Describe what happened, how it made you feel, and how you reacted at the time.

Questions to Consider:

- What were the circumstances surrounding this storm?
- How did you feel emotionally, mentally, and physically?
- What actions did you take in response to this challenge?

Step 2: Identify the Impact

Reflect on how each storm has impacted your life. Think about the changes it brought about, whether positive or negative. Write down these impacts next to each storm you described.

Questions to Consider:

- How did this storm change you as a person?

- Did it alter your perspective on life or certain situations?

- What immediate and long-term effects did it have on your life?

Step 3: Extract the Lessons

Now, focus on the lessons you learned from each storm. These lessons might be about yourself, others, or life in general. Write down the key takeaways from each experience.

Questions to Consider:

- What did you learn about your strengths and weaknesses?

- How did this storm reveal your values and priorities?

- What insights did you gain about relationships, work, or self-care?

Step 4: Apply the Lessons

Think about how you can apply these lessons to your current life and future challenges. Write down practical steps you can take to incorporate these insights into your daily routine.

Questions to Consider:

- How can you use these lessons to make better decisions?

- What changes can you make to avoid similar storms in the future?

- How can you use your experiences to help others facing similar challenges?

Step 5: Share Your Insights

If you feel comfortable, share your reflections and lessons with a trusted friend, family member, or mentor. Discussing your experiences can provide additional perspectives and reinforce the lessons you've learned.

Questions to Consider:

- Who can you share your story with to provide mutual support?

- How can sharing your experiences strengthen your relationships?

- What feedback or advice might you receive that could further your growth?

Step 6: Create a Lesson Plan

Turn your insights into a concrete plan. Create a "lesson plan" that outlines how you will implement these lessons moving forward. Set specific goals and timelines to track your progress.

Questions to Consider:

- What specific goals can you set to apply these lessons?

- What timeline will you follow to achieve these goals?

- How will you measure your progress and stay accountable?

Closing Reflection

After completing this activity, take a moment to reflect on the overall process. Consider the growth you've experienced and the strength you've gained from facing your storms. Remember, identifying and understanding your lessons is an ongoing journey, and each step brings you closer to a deeper understanding of yourself and God's purpose for your life.

Scripture for Reflection: "Consider it pure joy, my brothers and sisters, whenever you face trials of many kinds, because you know that the testing of your faith produces perseverance. Let perseverance finish its work so that you may be mature and complete, not lacking anything." – James 1:2-4

May this activity help you find clarity, strength, and purpose in the storms you face, and may you continue to grow in faith and resilience.

Moving Forward with Your Lessons from Hood Ships

Once you've identified the lessons from your life's storms and hood ships, the next step is to weave these insights into the fabric of your daily life. This means making conscious changes in your behaviors, thoughts, and routines to reflect what you've learned. Begin by setting aside time each week for reflection. This could be through journaling, meditation, or prayer. Reflect on how you've applied your lessons in various situations throughout the week. Ask yourself what went well and what could be improved.

Based on your lessons, set specific, achievable goals. For example, if you've learned the importance of self-care, you might set a goal to spend at least 30 minutes each day doing something that relaxes you. Write these goals down and review them regularly to track your progress. Remember, change begins in the mind. Work on developing a growth mindset, where challenges are seen as opportunities to learn and grow. Remind yourself of the lessons you've learned whenever you face a new challenge. Positive affirmations can be a powerful tool to reinforce this mindset. As Nelson Mandela once said, "I never lose. I either win or learn."

Turn your lessons into habits. If you've learned the value of setting boundaries, practice saying no to commitments that drain your energy. Consistency is key. The more you practice these new habits, the more they will become a natural part of your routine. Share your goals and the lessons you've learned with a trusted friend or mentor. They can provide support and hold you accountable, ensuring you stay on track. Regular check-ins can help you stay motivated and committed to your growth.

Using Your Lessons to Help Others

Your experiences and the lessons you've learned from navigating your hood ships can also be a source of inspiration and guidance for others. Sharing your journey can create a ripple effect, helping others navigate their own storms with greater wisdom and resilience. Be open about your experiences. Whether it's through social media, a blog, or in conversations with friends, sharing your story can provide comfort and encouragement to those going through similar struggles. Your vulnerability can be a powerful tool for connection and healing.

Look for opportunities to support others who might be facing similar challenges. This could be through volunteering, joining support groups, or simply being there for a friend in need. Use your lessons to offer practical advice and emotional support. If you're in a position to do so, consider mentoring someone who is going through a difficult time. Sharing the wisdom you've gained can help guide them through their own journey. Your insights and encouragement can make a significant difference in their life.

Use your experiences to advocate for changes that can benefit others. This could be through community involvement, raising awareness about important issues, or supporting organizations that align with the lessons you've learned. Your voice and actions can contribute to positive change. The most powerful way to influence others is by living out the lessons you've learned. Show through your actions how you've grown and changed. Your example can inspire others to reflect on their own experiences and make positive changes in their lives.

Realistic Examples

If you've learned the importance of setting boundaries, you might start by politely declining extra work assignments that overextend you. Instead, allocate that time to activities that recharge you, such as spending time with family or pursuing a hobby. Reflecting weekly on these decisions can help reinforce your commitment to self-care. Suppose your hood ship taught you the value of financial independence. Set a goal to create a budget and stick to it. Start saving a portion of your income each month. Review your financial goals regularly to ensure you're on track and make adjustments as needed.

If you discovered that failure is a part of growth, remind yourself of this lesson whenever you face setbacks. Instead of getting discouraged, view each setback as a learning opportunity. Affirmations like "I grow stronger with each challenge I face" can help solidify this mindset. If you learned the importance of healthy living, establish a routine that includes regular exercise and balanced nutrition. Make it a habit to prepare meals in advance and schedule workouts as non-negotiable parts of your day. Over time, these habits will become second nature.

Share your progress with a friend or mentor who can hold you accountable. For instance, if your goal is to improve your time management, have regular check-ins where you discuss your schedule and receive feedback. This external accountability can keep you motivated and on track.

By integrating the lessons you've learned from your hood ships into your daily life and using them to help others, you not only transform your own life but also create a positive impact on those around you. Reflect on your journey, set intentional goals, adjust your mindset, and build new habits that align with your growth. Share your story, offer support, mentor others, advocate for change, and lead by example. In doing so, you not only empower yourself but also inspire those around you to navigate their own storms with faith and resilience. Together, we can build a community rooted in understanding, compassion, and purposeful growth.

CHAPTER 9

"Harboring Hope:
A Hood Odyssey"

Scripture: Isaiah 43:2

This verse speaks of the abundant hope that comes from trusting in God. It emphasizes the joy and peace that believers can experience through the power of the Holy Spirit, instilling confidence in God's ability to bring about positive change.

When does hope start manifesting in your life? What's that saying about having the faith of a mustard seed? Listen, honey, this is how I look at hope. My hope has been so small it's almost nonexistent when it comes to certain parts of my life. Where do I start? This part might make me cry. I am thinking about my love life and my trust in some people now. Hope is difficult when people keep attacking the small ounce of hope you have left. I might ship this book to a few of them when I finish writing it. Let's deal with one at a time. After about 5-6 years of being single, I decided to seriously date again. Why did I do that? When I say I poured a large amount of energy into someone who was not giving me even 10% back, it's sad because I started to think that I was stupid. But the truth is that I get some weird high from supporting and motivating others, but this is not always good when the energy is not reciprocated.

Hope often starts as a fragile seed, barely noticeable amidst the chaos and challenges of life. It can be especially hard to maintain hope when you feel like you're constantly giving and never receiving. I've been there, investing time, energy, and love into relationships that were more draining than fulfilling. The hardest part was realizing that I was the one who allowed my hope to be chipped away by people who didn't value me.

One of the lessons I've learned is that hope isn't about expecting others to change; it's about nurturing the belief that you deserve better and trusting God to lead you to it. When I started dating again, I hoped for a meaningful connection. Instead, I found myself in a one-sided relationship that left me feeling depleted. This experience taught me that hope must be coupled with discernment. We can't allow ourselves to hope blindly; we must also seek God's wisdom in our decisions.

Romans 15:13 reminds us that true hope comes from God and is accompanied by joy and peace. It's not about the circumstances around us but about the confidence we have in God's promises. When I felt my hope dwindling, I turned to prayer and scripture, asking God to restore my spirit and fill me with His peace. It wasn't an overnight transformation, but slowly, I felt my hope rekindling, stronger and more resilient.

Hope isn't passive; it requires action. I began setting boundaries and distancing myself from relationships that drained me. I started focusing on my passions and dreams, things that brought me joy and fulfillment. This shift in focus helped me see that hope thrives when we invest in ourselves and our God-given purpose. It's about finding joy in the journey, even when the destination isn't clear.

For example, think about the story of Joseph in the Bible. Despite being sold into slavery and imprisoned unjustly, Joseph never lost hope. He trusted that God had a plan for him, even in the darkest times. His unwavering hope and faith eventually led him to a position of great power, where he could save many lives. Joseph's story teaches us that hope, when anchored in God, can carry us through the most challenging storms.

Reflecting on my own hood odyssey, I realize that hope has been a constant companion, even when it felt like it was barely there. It was hope that pushed me to keep trying, to keep loving, and to keep believing in a better future. It was hope that reminded me that I am worthy of love and respect, and that God's plans for me are good.

Hope is also about community. Surrounding ourselves with people who uplift and encourage us can make a huge difference. When I shared my struggles with trusted friends and mentors, their support and wisdom helped me see my situation in a new light. They reminded me of my worth and encouraged me to keep hoping and trusting in God's plan.

It's important to remember that hope isn't just about the big things. It's found in the small, everyday moments of joy and peace. It's in the laughter with friends, the quiet moments of prayer, and the simple pleasures that bring us happiness. By focusing on these moments, we can nurture our hope and keep it alive, even in the face of adversity.

Remember, harboring hope in the midst of life's storms and hood ships is a journey of faith and resilience. It requires us to trust in God, nurture our spirits, and surround ourselves with positive influences. By doing so, we can keep our hope alive and strong, guiding us through the challenges and leading us to a brighter, more fulfilling future.

The other issue that I am faced with takes more to focus on the word support. This year, I decided to focus more on my brand and invest in my business growth. I've had countless events and made some good and bad connections over the years. I am at a point where my hope is diminishing. Recently, I hired someone to help with building my brand, and instead, they seemed more interested in taking my money than delivering the promised services. The truth is, I have grown tired of wanting to genuinely support people who do not want to support themselves or others. These people put on facades and play the victim at every turn. I had to separate myself and remove her access to me before she took me down. I had to ask God to guide me and my words as I dealt with this situation. Instead of providing her with choice words, I decided to offer her constructive criticism as I basically lost money and wasted time with her pretend services. I was proud of myself for not losing control as I had thought of doing many times, but instead, I let God handle it. With that being said, let's pray for her now. Remember, yes, this might be shade, but I am not perfect and God is working on me.

Focusing on building my brand has been a journey filled with both hope and disappointment. The hope of growing my business and reaching new heights has kept me motivated, but the setbacks and dishonesty from others have often left me questioning my path. It's hard to maintain hope when you feel taken advantage of, but it's in these moments that we must lean into our faith even more.

Supporting others who don't reciprocate can be exhausting and disheartening. It can make you question your own worth and intentions. However, I realized that my support for others shouldn't come at the cost of my own well-being and progress. It's important to recognize when to step back and reassess the situation. Sometimes, the most loving thing you can do for yourself is to set boundaries and remove toxic influences from your life.

In Romans 15:13, we are reminded that God is the source of our hope, filling us with joy and peace as we trust in Him. This verse has been a guiding light for me, especially in times when my hope seems to wane. By trusting in God and His plan, I find the strength to continue moving forward, even when the path is uncertain.

Learning to navigate the business world with integrity and faith has been a significant part of my hood odyssey. Each setback is a lesson, a chance to grow and become wiser. It's about finding the balance between supporting others and ensuring that you're also taking care of your own needs. Sometimes, it means making tough decisions and trusting that God will guide you through the process.

The experience of hiring someone who didn't meet my expectations was a harsh lesson in discernment. It taught me to be more cautious and to trust my instincts. It also reinforced the importance of surrounding myself with people who genuinely want to see me succeed and who share my values. This journey is about building a community that uplifts and supports one another, reflecting the true essence of hood ships.

Hope in business, as in life, requires resilience. It's about bouncing back from disappointments and continuing to pursue your dreams with unwavering faith. Each challenge faced is an opportunity to refine your approach and strengthen your resolve. It's a reminder that God's plan for us is always greater than what we can envision for ourselves.

As I continue to build my brand, I hold onto the hope that God places in my heart. This hope drives me to push through the tough times and to celebrate the victories, no matter how small. It's a journey of faith, trust, and perseverance, knowing that with God, all things are possible.

In the end, hope is what sustains us through the trials and tribulations of our hood odyssey. It's what keeps us moving forward, even when the road is rough. By holding onto hope and trusting in God's plan, we can navigate any storm and come out stronger on the other side. As we reflect on our journey through the storms and the lessons learned, let us find solace and inspiration in these words:

In the midst of storms and troubled seas,

Hope remains our guiding breeze.

Through hood ships' trials, fierce and grand,

God's steady hand will help us stand.

Though friends may falter, and plans may break,

In God's great love, we'll find no mistake.

Each setback, a lesson, each hurdle, a test,

In faith, we'll persevere, in hope, we'll rest.

Our dreams may waver, our strength may sway,

But trust in God will light our way.

For every loss, there's a greater gain,

Through every tear, a lesson's name.

So hold on tight to hope's bright flame,

For in God's grace, we'll find our name.

With every dawn, a new chance to start,

With hope in our soul, and faith

SOMETHING HAS TO GIVE

Prompt Questions:

1. Reflect on a time when you felt overwhelmed by a situation or relationship. What were the signs that indicated something needed to change? How did you respond, and what did you learn from that experience?

2. Consider a current challenge you are facing. What steps can you take to address this issue and make a positive change? How can you invite God's guidance into this process?

Prayer: Dear Heavenly Father, we come before You, acknowledging the moments when we feel overwhelmed and burdened by life's challenges. We ask for Your wisdom and guidance to help us recognize when something has to give. Grant us the courage to make necessary changes and the strength to let go of what no longer serves Your purpose for our lives. Fill us with Your peace and assurance, knowing that You are with us every step of the way. Help us to trust in Your plan and to seek Your will in all that we do. In Jesus' name, we pray. Amen.

Affirmations:

- *I trust in God's guidance to lead me through challenging times.*

- *I am courageous and willing to make necessary changes for my well-being.*

- *I release what no longer serves me and embrace God's plan for my life.*

- *I am strong and capable of navigating life's storms with faith and resilience.*

- *I invite God's wisdom and peace into every aspect of my life.*

- *I am worthy of healthy and supportive relationships that align with my purpose.*

- *I choose to prioritize my well-being and set boundaries that honor my needs.*

- *I am open to growth and transformation, trusting that God is working all things for my good.*

- *I find strength in my faith and confidence in God's unwavering love.*

- *I am resilient and capable of overcoming any challenge with God's help.*

CHAPTER 10

"Tides of Transformation: My Journey with God and Hood Ships"

Scripture: 2 Corinthians 5:17

This verse speaks of the transformative power of God's grace. It signifies the renewal and regeneration experienced by those who are in Christ, illustrating the profound change that occurs in a believer's life through their journey with God.

Transformation: The process of profound and significant change that fundamentally alters one's character, perspective, or condition. It involves a deep and enduring shift in beliefs, behaviors, and attitudes, often leading to personal growth, renewal, and a greater alignment with one's true purpose and potential. Transformation can be spiritual, emotional, physical, or intellectual, resulting in a new state of being that reflects a higher understanding and connection to oneself, others, and the divine.

Phew, I feel like that definition was a word within itself. Do you feel like transformation happens to you daily? I know that I do. It's like I am always striving to be the future me, working on embracing all parts of who I am developing into. As I am writing, I am thinking, "Girl, what are you about to say?" See, I must be going through a transformation at this very moment. Honey, hold on. God, I have a question: when will this transformation process end? Because I am tired of change. That was meant to make you laugh. Okay, change and transformation are necessary for your growth.

Let me go back to this dead horse that I am beating, but when someone shows you who they are, believe them. And when the season is done for that hood ship, baby, it is done. Moving from that, you have to use that word discernment in real life, and you have to stay one step ahead of those individuals who want to hold on to a relationship with you only for their personal gain and no benefit to you. God wants you to have genuine relationships and people who care about your well-being too.

Transformation isn't a one-time event; it's a continuous journey. Every day, we are presented with new challenges, opportunities, and lessons that shape who we are becoming. It's like the process of refining gold – each trial, each struggle, and each victory brings out more of our true value. Embracing transformation means being open to change and trusting that God is molding us into something beautiful.

Reflecting on my own journey, I realize that every hood ship I've experienced has been a catalyst for transformation. Whether it was a friendship that ended or a job that didn't work out, each experience taught me something valuable about myself and God's plan for my life. These experiences pushed me out of my comfort zone and into a place where I could grow and develop.

Sometimes, transformation requires us to let go of what's familiar and comfortable. It means stepping into the unknown with faith, trusting that God has something better in store for us. It's in these moments of uncertainty that we often find our greatest strength. The process can be painful, but it's necessary for our growth and development.

One of the key aspects of transformation is discernment. It's about recognizing when a relationship or situation is no longer serving your highest good and having the courage to let it go. It's about trusting that God will bring the right people and opportunities into your life at the right time. Discernment helps us navigate the tides of transformation with wisdom and grace.

Transformation also involves embracing our true selves. It means acknowledging our flaws and imperfections and understanding that they are part of our unique journey. God doesn't ask us to be perfect; He asks us to be authentic. By embracing who we are, we can fully step into the purpose He has for us.

In the midst of transformation, it's important to surround ourselves with people who support and uplift us. These are the individuals who will stand by us through the highs and lows, offering encouragement and wisdom. Genuine relationships are a crucial part of our journey, helping us stay grounded and focused on our growth.

As we navigate the tides of transformation, we must remember that God is always with us. He is our constant source of strength and guidance. When we feel overwhelmed or uncertain, we can turn to Him for comfort and reassurance. His love and grace are the anchors that keep us steady in the midst of change.

Reflect on your own journey of transformation. What lessons have you learned? How have you grown and changed over the years? Embrace these experiences as part of your unique story, and trust that God is leading you toward greater things. Each step you take is a step closer to becoming the person He created you to be.

Understand that transformation is an ongoing process that requires faith, courage, and discernment. It's about letting go of the old and embracing the new, trusting that God's plan for us is good. As we continue on this journey, let's hold onto the hope and promise found in 2 Corinthians 5:17 – "The old has gone, the new is here!" With God by our side, we can navigate the tides of transformation and emerge stronger, wiser, and more aligned with our true purpose.

Mirror of Reflection

Lalah Hathaway's song "Mirror" is a profound reminder of the importance of self-reflection in the journey of transformation. The lyrics encourage us to look in the mirror and face our true selves, embracing both our strengths and weaknesses. This process of self-reflection is crucial for personal growth. By honestly assessing our actions, motivations, and beliefs, we can identify areas that need change and work towards becoming the best version of ourselves. This song has gotten me through many tough days, serving as a constant reminder of the power of self-awareness and the importance of authenticity.

The song's message aligns with James 1:23-24, which states, "Anyone who listens to the word but does not do what it says is like someone who looks at his face in a mirror and, after looking at himself, goes away and immediately forgets what he looks like." This scripture emphasizes the importance of not just hearing God's word but also applying it to our lives. Self-reflection allows us to see where we are falling short and make necessary adjustments.

In the context of hood ships, reflecting on our relationships and their impact on our lives is essential. Are these relationships helping us grow, or are they holding us back? Just like looking in a mirror, we need to examine these connections and decide whether they align with our values and goals. This honest assessment can be difficult but is necessary for genuine transformation.

Moreover, self-reflection helps us understand our role in the dynamics of our relationships. Are we contributing positively, or are we part of the problem? By looking in the mirror, we can identify patterns of behavior that need to change. This process requires humility and a willingness to accept our imperfections, but it is a crucial step in the journey of transformation.

Finally, "Mirror" reminds us that transformation starts from within. Before we can change our external circumstances, we must first change ourselves. This internal work involves confronting our fears, insecurities, and past mistakes. By doing so, we can move forward with a clearer sense of purpose and a stronger foundation of self-awareness.

Building Bridges, Not Walls

Transformation often involves building bridges instead of walls. It's about creating connections that foster growth and understanding rather than isolating ourselves from others. The Bible encourages us to be peacemakers and bridge-builders, promoting unity and reconciliation in our relationships.

In Matthew 5:9, Jesus says, "Blessed are the peacemakers, for they will be called children of God." This scripture highlights the importance of actively seeking peace and harmony in our interactions. Building bridges means reaching out to others, even those with whom we may have conflicts, and working towards mutual understanding and forgiveness.

Think about the movie "Remember the Titans." The film is a powerful example of how building bridges can transform a community. The story revolves around a high school football team in Virginia during the early 1970s, a time of racial tension and integration. Through the leadership of their coach and the willingness of the players to bridge their differences, the team not only succeeds on the field but also unites their community.

In our own lives, we are often faced with opportunities to build bridges. Whether it's mending a broken relationship, fostering a new connection, or promoting understanding in a divided environment, these actions require courage and intentionality. By focusing on common ground and shared values, we can create relationships that are stronger and more resilient.

Building bridges also means being open to learning from others. Each person we encounter has unique experiences and perspectives that can enrich our own understanding. By listening and empathizing, we can gain insights that contribute to our personal growth and transformation.

Moreover, building bridges aligns with the concept of hood ships. It's about creating relationships that support and uplift us, rather than those that isolate and diminish us. By fostering connections based on mutual respect and shared purpose, we can navigate life's challenges more effectively and experience the true power of community.

From Pain to Purpose

One of the most profound aspects of transformation is the ability to turn pain into purpose. The trials and tribulations we face can be incredibly difficult, but they also have the potential to shape us into stronger, more compassionate individuals. Romans 8:28 reminds us, "And we know that in all things God works for the good of those who love him, who have been called according to his purpose."

This verse reassures us that even our most painful experiences can be used for good. Our struggles can become the foundation for our greatest strengths. By finding purpose in our pain, we can transform our suffering into a source of inspiration and motivation for ourselves and others.

Consider the story of J.K. Rowling, the author of the Harry Potter series. Before achieving worldwide success, Rowling faced numerous rejections from publishers, financial struggles, and personal hardships. Despite these challenges, she persevered and used her experiences to fuel her writing. Her story is a testament to the power of turning pain into purpose.

In the context of hood ships, we often face situations that test our resilience and faith. These experiences, though painful, can lead us to a deeper understanding of ourselves and our purpose. By reflecting on our challenges and seeking God's guidance, we can find meaning in our suffering and use it to propel us forward.

Transformation requires us to embrace our pain and see it as a catalyst for growth. It means acknowledging our struggles and using them to fuel our journey toward healing and wholeness. By turning our pain into purpose, we can create a narrative of strength and perseverance that inspires others.

Moreover, finding purpose in our pain helps us develop empathy and compassion for others. When we understand the depth of our own struggles, we are better equipped to support those going through similar experiences. Our pain becomes a bridge that connects us to others, fostering a sense of community and shared understanding.

As we navigate the tides of transformation, let us remember that our pain is not in vain. It is a crucial part of our journey, shaping us into the individuals we are meant to be. By embracing our pain and finding purpose in it, we can transform our lives and the lives of those around us.

SOMETHING HAS TO GIVE

Life often brings us to a breaking point where we realize that something has to give. We can't keep carrying the weight of toxic relationships, self-doubt, and unmet expectations. It's in these moments of realization that we find the courage to make necessary changes and let go of what no longer serves us.

Maya Angelou once said, "You may not control all the events that happen to you, but you can decide not to be reduced by them." This powerful quote reminds us that while we can't control everything that happens in our lives, we can choose how we respond. We can choose to rise above our circumstances and not let them define us.

So, what will you do when you reach that point where something has to give? Will you hold on to what's comfortable but harmful, or will you take the bold step to release and transform? Remember, transformation begins with a single decision to change.

Prompt Question: What is one area of your life where you feel something has to give? What steps can you take today to begin making a positive change in that area?

Let us Pray: Heavenly Father, we come to You in moments of struggle and realization, knowing that something in our lives has to give. Grant us the courage to let go of what no longer serves us and the wisdom to embrace change with an open heart. Help us to trust in Your guidance and lean on Your strength as we navigate these challenging times. Fill us with Your peace and assurance that even when we cannot see the way forward, You are leading us toward a brighter future. Lord, transform our pain into purpose and our struggles into strength. We surrender our fears and doubts to You, believing that Your plans for us are good and that You will bring us through every storm. In Jesus' name, we pray. Amen.

Affirmations:

- I am worthy of healthy, fulfilling relationships.

- I have the strength to let go of what no longer serves me.

- God is guiding me through every change and transformation.

- I trust in the process of growth and renewal.

- My life is filled with purpose and potential.

- I embrace change as a pathway to greater things.

- I am resilient and capable of overcoming any challenge.

- God's love and grace empower me to make positive changes.

- I am surrounded by supportive and uplifting relationships.

- My future is bright, and I am confident in God's plan for my life.

By reflecting on these affirmations and incorporating them into your daily routine, you can reinforce your commitment to positive change and transformation. Remember, the journey may be challenging, but with God by your side, you have the strength to overcome and thrive.

CHAPTER 11

"Single Motherhood: Navigating Hood Ships with Strength and Faith"

Scripture: Isaiah 41:10 (NIV)

"Do not fear, for I am with you; do not be dismayed, for I am your God. I will strengthen you and help you; I will uphold you with my righteous right hand."

Navigating the hood ships of single motherhood is one of the most challenging yet rewarding journeys I have ever embarked on. There are days when the weight of responsibility feels overwhelming, but it is in these moments that I am reminded of Isaiah 41:10: "Do not fear, for I am with you; do not be dismayed, for I am your God. I will strengthen you and help you; I will uphold you with my righteous right hand." This verse has been my anchor, reminding me that I am never alone in this journey.

I debated whether to include this chapter about my journey or hood ship as a single mother. I am not trying to say that it is not challenging to be a parent, but single motherhood adds another layer of complexity. I've encountered people, some I thought were friends, who crossed the line with conversations about how I should parent or tried to downplay the overwhelming challenge and balance it takes to be a successful single-parent. God, let me stop and thank You for giving me such amazing sons, who for the most part didn't make things harder for me.

The truth is, honestly, I still was tired and resented their father for not having to be an effective parent and involved. Once I got past that, I found that the biggest success and joy I have found was being my sons' mother. This is one of the best hood ships that I have. There is nothing I can say to describe how proud I am of my sons, one with his standing 4.0 GPA and the other who recently graduated from high school, beating the odds against young Black men.

Reflecting on my early days as a single mother, I remember the fear and uncertainty that clouded my thoughts, after starting over with two children following an abusive marriage. Each day felt like a new battle, but I learned to rely on God's strength and wisdom to guide me. Isaiah 41:10 became my lifeline, a constant reminder that God was with me, even in the darkest moments. This verse reassured me that I was not alone and that God would provide the strength and support I needed to navigate this challenging journey.

One of the most significant challenges I faced was balancing work and parenting. As a single mother, I had to be both the breadwinner and the caregiver. This dual role often left me exhausted and overwhelmed, but I found solace in prayer and faith. I learned to lean on God for strength and guidance, trusting that He would help me manage my responsibilities. Over time, I discovered that God's grace was sufficient for me, providing the endurance and resilience I needed to keep going.

Another challenge was dealing with societal judgments and stereotypes. As a single mother, I often felt scrutinized and judged by others who did not understand my struggles. There were times when I questioned my worth and abilities as a parent, but I learned to find my identity in Christ rather than in the opinions of others. God's word reminded me that I was fearfully and wonderfully made, and that His plans for me were good. This realization gave me the confidence to rise above the negativity and focus on being the best mother I could be.

Building a strong support system was crucial for my journey as a single mother. I surrounded myself with friends and family who uplifted and encouraged me. Their support provided much-needed relief and reminded me that I was not alone. Ecclesiastes 4:9-10 emphasizes the value of companionship and mutual support, and I experienced this firsthand. Having people who believed in me and my abilities as a mother made a significant difference in my journey.

I also learned the importance of self-care. As a single mother, it was easy to neglect my own needs while focusing on my children's well-being. However, I realized that taking care of myself was essential for being a good mother. I made time for activities that rejuvenated me, such as reading, exercising, and spending time in nature. This self-care allowed me to recharge and be more present and patient with my children.

One of the most rewarding aspects of single motherhood has been watching my sons grow and thrive. Despite the challenges we faced, they have excelled in their academics and personal lives. My youngest son, with his impeccable 4.0 GPA, and oldest, who recently graduated from high school against the odds, are living testaments to God's faithfulness. Their achievements bring me immense joy and pride, and I am grateful for the privilege of being their mother.

In addition to academic success, I have seen my sons develop into compassionate and resilient individuals. They have learned the value of hard work, perseverance, and faith. Witnessing their growth and maturity has been a source of encouragement and affirmation that God's hand has been upon us throughout our journey. Their success is a testament to the power of faith, love, and determination.

As I reflect on our journey, I am reminded of the importance of gratitude. Despite the hardships, there have been countless blessings along the way. I am grateful for the strength and wisdom that God has provided, for the support of friends and family, and for the moments of joy and triumph. Gratitude has been a powerful tool in shifting my perspective and finding contentment in the midst of challenges.

Looking ahead, I am excited about the future and the opportunities that lie ahead for my sons and me. I am confident that with God's continued guidance and support, we will continue to overcome obstacles and achieve our dreams. Single motherhood has been a journey of growth and transformation, and I am grateful for every lesson learned and every blessing received.

Navigating the hood ships of single motherhood has been both challenging and rewarding. Through faith, resilience, and the support of loved ones, I have learned to overcome obstacles and find joy in the journey. Isaiah 41:10 has been my anchor, reminding me that God is with me every step of the way. As I look back on our journey, I am filled with gratitude and hope for the future. My sons and I are living proof that with God's strength, we can weather any storm and emerge stronger on the other side.

Strength Through Faith

Navigating single motherhood requires a deep reservoir of strength, and for me, that strength has come from my unwavering faith in God. Every morning, as I faced the challenges of raising my sons alone, I would turn to prayer and scripture for guidance. Isaiah 41:10 was a constant source of comfort, reminding me that God was with me and would provide the strength I needed. This assurance allowed me to face each day with renewed courage, knowing that I was not alone in my journey.

There were times when my faith was tested, especially during moments of financial strain, such as our power being cut off or emotional exhaustion. But each time I felt myself weakening, I would remind myself of God's promises. His words gave me the resilience to push through, to find solutions, and to keep moving forward for the sake of my sons. My faith became a shield against the worries and fears that threatened to overwhelm me.

Faith also played a crucial role in teaching my sons about the power of belief and trust in God. By witnessing my reliance on God, they learned the importance of turning to Him in times of need. This foundation of faith has not only strengthened our bond as a family but also equipped them with the spiritual tools they need to navigate their own challenges.

Prompt Questions:

- How has your faith helped you navigate the challenges of single parenthood?

- In what ways can you incorporate more faith-based practices into your daily routine?

Affirmations:

- I am strong because I trust in God's promises.

- My faith provides me with the resilience to face any challenge.

Building a Support Network

One of the most important lessons I've learned as a single mother is the value of a strong support network. Initially, I tried to do everything on my own, believing that asking for help was a sign of weakness. However, I soon realized that even the strongest among us need a village. Surrounding myself with friends, family, and a faith community provided the support I needed to thrive.

My parents, Carl, Tracy, Shana, and Tim played a pivotal role in this support network. Their encouragement and practical help were invaluable, allowing me to balance work and parenting responsibilities. They stepped in during times of crisis, providing a safety net that caught me when I stumbled. Their unwavering support reminded me that I was never truly alone, even in my hardest moments.

Beyond family, I also found solace in the companionship of close friends. My best friends became my confidants, offering a listening ear and practical advice. They reminded me to take care of myself and encouraged me to pursue my dreams despite the challenges This network of support was a testament to Proverbs 27:17, which underscores the importance of companionship and mutual support: "As iron sharpens iron, so one person sharpens another."

Prompt Questions:

- Who are the key people in your support network, and how have they helped you?

- What steps can you take to strengthen your support system?

Affirmations:

- I am surrounded by people who love and support me.

- My support network is a source of strength and encouragement.

Embracing Self-Care

Amidst the hustle and bustle of single motherhood, self-care often fell by the wayside. However, I soon learned that neglecting my own needs only made the journey more difficult. Embracing self-care became essential for maintaining my physical, emotional, and spiritual well-being. It wasn't easy, but it was necessary.

I began to carve out time for activities that rejuvenated me. Whether it was a quiet moment of reflection, a long walk in nature, or indulging in a good book, these small acts of self-care made a significant difference. They allowed me to recharge and approach my responsibilities with a clear mind and a positive attitude. Self-care became a way to honor myself and acknowledge the hard work I was putting into raising my sons.

Music also played a vital role in my self-care routine. Lalah Hathaway's "Mirror" became an anthem for me, a reminder to reflect on my journey and appreciate the progress I had made. This song helped me through many tough days, offering a sense of solace and encouragement. It reminded me to look in the mirror and see the strength and resilience within me.

Incorporating these self-care practices into my daily routine wasn't always easy, but it was a crucial step in maintaining my well-being. By taking care of myself, I was better equipped to take care of my sons and navigate the challenges of single motherhood. Self-care wasn't a luxury; it was a necessity that allowed me to be the best version of myself for my family.

Prompt Questions:

- What self-care practices can you incorporate into your daily routine?

- How does taking care of yourself impact your ability to care for others?

Affirmations:

- I deserve time for myself to recharge and rejuvenate.

- Self-care is a vital part of my well-being and my ability to support my family.

SOMETHING HAS TO GIVE

As single mothers, we often find ourselves stretched to the limit, juggling numerous responsibilities and constantly giving to others. However, it's crucial to recognize when something has to give. Understanding our limits and knowing when to say no is essential for maintaining our health and well-being. We can't pour from an empty cup, and taking on too much can lead to burnout and resentment.

Setting boundaries is an act of self-respect and self-preservation. It's about prioritizing our needs and recognizing that we can't do everything. Learning to delegate tasks and accept help is vital. It's okay to admit that we need a break and to take time for ourselves without feeling guilty. Remember, by taking care of ourselves, we are better equipped to care for our children.

One famous quote by Brené Brown resonates deeply with this concept: "Daring to set boundaries is about having the courage to love ourselves, even when we risk disappointing others." This reminds us that our well-being should come first, and it's okay to disappoint others if it means taking care of ourselves.

Let us pray: Dear God, grant me the strength to recognize my limits and the wisdom to set boundaries that protect my well-being. Help me to prioritize my needs and accept help when necessary. Give me the courage to say no when I need to and to take time for myself without guilt. Thank you for the support network you've provided and for your constant presence in my life. Amen.

Affirmations:

- I have the courage to set boundaries that protect my well-being.

- It's okay to say no and prioritize my needs.

By incorporating these practices and reflections into your life, you can navigate the challenges of single motherhood with strength, faith, and resilience. Embrace your journey, trust in God's guidance, and remember that you are never alone in this path. You are doing an incredible job, and with each step, you are moving closer to the life you envision for yourself and your children.

CHAPTER 12

"Anchoring Down:
Final Reflections on Hood Ships"

Scripture: Hebrews 6:19 (NIV)
"We have this hope as an anchor for the soul, firm and secure. It enters the inner sanctuary behind the curtain."

This scripture speaks of the steadfast hope we have in God, which serves as an anchor for our souls. In the context of hood ships, this hope and faith in God's promises provide stability and security amidst life's storms. Just as an anchor holds a ship steady, our hope in God grounds us, keeping us firm and secure even when the waves of life threaten to overwhelm us.

Here we go back to this anchor situation that we led with in the beginning. Like a ship navigating through the waves, we seek to find a smooth flow on our ride. The truth is that hood ships might be smooth at one point and shaky the next moment. Most of the hood ships shared started off positive and felt good, but they led to what we would consider a disastrous end filled with pain, tears, and a lack of hope.

As we reflect on the various hood ships we've encountered, it's important to recognize that these experiences are a part of our growth journey. They are the storms that test our resilience and faith. The rough seas we face are not meant to break us but to mold us into stronger individuals. Each storm, each wave that crashes against us, shapes us and builds our character.

Hope serves as our anchor, keeping us grounded and firm. It is this hope that allows us to stand tall in the face of adversity. Just as a ship relies on its anchor to remain steady, we rely on our hope in God to stay grounded. This hope is not just a fleeting feeling but a profound assurance of God's unwavering love and guidance.

Hebrews 6:19 reminds us that our hope is firm and secure, entering the inner sanctuary behind the curtain. This imagery speaks to the depth and strength of our faith. Our hope is not superficial; it is deeply rooted in the promises of God. It penetrates the deepest parts of our souls, providing us with a sense of peace and security.

Throughout this book, we have explored the highs and lows of hood ships, from the moments of joy and connection to the times of heartbreak and pain. These experiences have taught us valuable lessons about ourselves and our relationships. They have shown us the importance of discerning who we let into our lives and the necessity of setting boundaries to protect our well-being.

Reflecting on my own journey, I remember times when I felt adrift, tossed about by the storms of life. I questioned my worth and doubted my ability to navigate the turbulent waters. But it was during these times of uncertainty that I clung to my hope in God. It was this hope that kept me anchored and gave me the strength to keep moving forward.

One of the most profound realizations I had was the importance of building meaningful, purposeful relationships. Proverbs 17:17 stays that "A friend loves at all times, and a brother is born for a time of adversity."True relationships uplift and support us, helping us navigate the challenges of life with grace and strength. These relationships act as our support system, providing encouragement, wisdom, and accountability.

However, not all relationships are meant to last forever. Some people come into our lives for a season, serving a specific purpose before moving on. It's okay to let go of relationships that no longer align with our growth and purpose. Holding onto these relationships out of habit or fear can hinder our progress and keep us stuck in the past.

As we conclude our reflections on hood ships, let us remember that our journey is anchored in the hope and faith we have in God. No matter what storms we face, we can find peace and stability in knowing that God is our anchor. He holds us steady, guides us through the turbulent waters, and leads us to calmer seas. This hope allows us to face the future with confidence, knowing that with God by our side, we can overcome any challenge and emerge stronger and more resilient.

The story of Jesus calming the storm in Mark 4:39 is a powerful reminder of the peace and calm that Jesus can bring into our lives. He rebuked the wind and said to the waves, "Quiet! Be still!" Then the wind died down, and it was completely calm. Jesus asked His disciples, "Why are you so afraid? Do you still have no faith?" This passage reminds us that no matter how fierce the storm, Jesus has the power to bring peace and calm.

Just as in that passage, we must have faith that God is with us in our storms. It's easy to feel abandoned and lost when we're facing hardships, but Isaiah 43:2 reassures us that we will not be consumed by the flames. God is our protector and guide, even when we can't see the way forward.

Moreover, these storms teach us the importance of self-care. We can't pour from an empty cup. When I was overwhelmed with my job and the trauma it brought, I neglected my own needs. I had to learn to set boundaries and take care of myself first. This was crucial in finding balance and maintaining my mental health.

Self-care isn't just about taking breaks; it's about recognizing our worth and understanding that we deserve to be treated with kindness and respect. It's about making choices that align with our values and well-being. Sometimes, this means making difficult decisions, like leaving a toxic job or ending a harmful relationship.

In the end, the storms we face are not meant to destroy us but to refine us. They push us to grow, to trust in God more deeply, and to make changes that align with His plan for our lives. Remember Hebrews 6:19 and hold on to the promise that we will not be consumed. With God by our side, we can navigate any storm and come out stronger on the other side.

As we anchor down and reflect on our journey, let us embrace the lessons learned and the growth experienced. Let us move forward with hope, faith, and a renewed sense of purpose, knowing that God is our anchor, and with Him, we are never alone.

Embracing the Calm After the Storm

After navigating through the storms of life, it's essential to embrace the calm that follows. This is a time for reflection, healing, and growth. It's an opportunity to look back at the challenges we've overcome and recognize the strength and resilience we've gained. This calm period allows us to recharge and prepare for future challenges with renewed vigor.

In this season of calm, take the time to nurture your spirit. Engage in activities that bring you joy and peace. Whether it's spending time in nature, connecting with loved ones, or pursuing a hobby, these moments of tranquility are crucial for your well-being. Remember, it's in the stillness that we often hear God's voice most clearly.

Building Stronger Foundations

As we move forward, it's important to build stronger foundations for our relationships. Use the lessons learned from past hood ships to create healthier, more meaningful connections. This involves setting clear boundaries, communicating openly, and prioritizing mutual respect and support.

Consider the relationships that have stood the test of time and those that have not. Reflect on what made the lasting relationships strong and what caused others to falter. Use this insight to guide you in building future relationships that are based on trust, love, and a shared commitment to growth.

Looking Ahead with Hope

Finally, as we anchor down and reflect on our journey, let's look ahead with hope. The future is filled with endless possibilities, and with God's guidance, we can navigate whatever comes our way. Embrace the hope that Hebrews 6:19 speaks of, and let it be the anchor that keeps you steady.

Remember that every challenge faced and every storm weathered has a purpose. They shape us, teach us, and prepare us for greater things. Trust in God's plan for your life, and remain steadfast in your faith. With God as your anchor, you are equipped to handle any storm and emerge stronger on the other side.

4. **Reflect on Your Growth:**

   - How have the challenges you've faced in your hood ships shaped you as a person?

   - In what ways have you grown spiritually, emotionally, and mentally through these experiences?

5. **Evaluate Your Relationships:**

   - Are the relationships in your life uplifting and supporting you, or are they draining your energy?

   - What steps can you take to surround yourself with more positive, purposeful relationships?

6. **Set Intentional Goals:**

   - What lessons have you learned from your hood ships that you can apply to your future goals?

   - How can you ensure that your goals align with your values and purpose?

7. **Practice Self-Care and Self-Love:**

   - What self-care practices can you incorporate into your daily routine to maintain your well-being?

   - How can you show yourself more compassion and kindness as you navigate life's challenges?

8. **Trust in God's Guidance:**

   - How can you strengthen your faith and trust in God's plan for your life?

   - In what ways can you seek God's guidance more actively in your decision-making process?

Reflecting on these questions can help you gain deeper insights into your journey and guide you towards a more intentional and purposeful life. Remember, every step you take is part of your transformation and growth.

Let us Pray: Heavenly Father, as we anchor down and reflect on our journey, we thank You for the lessons learned and the strength gained. Help us to embrace the calm after the storm, to build stronger foundations in our relationships, and to look ahead with hope. May we always remember that You are our anchor, keeping us steady and secure. Guide us, protect us, and lead us to the bright future You have planned for us. In Jesus' name, we pray. Amen.

EPILOGUE

As I reflect on this journey through the intricate and often tumultuous waters of hood ships, I am reminded of the many lessons learned and the transformation experienced. From the early days of grappling with relationships and seeking clarity, to the profound moments of self-discovery and divine guidance, this journey has been nothing short of transformative.

Navigating life's challenges, much like sailing through a storm, requires faith, resilience, and a willingness to embrace change. It involves letting go of what no longer serves us and trusting that God's plan for our lives is far greater than we can imagine. Through the highs and lows, the joys and sorrows, we come to understand the true meaning of hope, trust, and transformation.

As I wrote each chapter of this book, I poured my heart into sharing the lessons and experiences that have shaped me. From the struggles of letting go of toxic relationships to the triumphs of finding purpose in pain, this journey has been a testament to the power of faith and the strength that lies within us.

I think back to the various hood ships that have come and gone, each one leaving an indelible mark on my soul. The moments of self-reflection, the times when I had to lean on God's guidance, and the instances where I saw His hand at work in my life have all contributed to the person I am today.

One of the most profound realizations has been the importance of building meaningful, purposeful relationships. Ecclesiastes 4:9-10 reminds us of the value of companionship and mutual support, and it's a lesson that has resonated deeply with me. True relationships uplift and support us, helping us navigate the challenges of life with grace and strength.

There were times when I felt like giving up, when the storms seemed too fierce and the journey too daunting. But it was in those moments that I discovered the depth of God's love and the power of His grace. He carried me through the darkest times, turning my pain into purpose and my trials into triumphs.

I am reminded of the words of Maya Angelou, "You may not control all the events that happen to you, but you can decide not to be reduced by them." This quote encapsulates the essence of this journey. We may face storms and challenges, but we have the power to rise above them and emerge stronger.

As you read this book, my hope is that you find inspiration and encouragement in these stories and lessons. May you be reminded that you are not alone in your struggles and that God's presence is always with you, guiding you toward a brighter future. Embrace the journey, trust in the process, and know that transformation is possible for all of us.

Let us pray: Heavenly Father, as we conclude this journey together, we thank You for the lessons learned and the transformation experienced. Grant us the strength to continue embracing change and the courage to let go of what no longer serves us. Help us to trust in Your plan for our lives and to lean on Your guidance through every storm. May we build meaningful, purposeful relationships that uplift and support us, and may we always remember the depth of Your love and grace. In Jesus' name, we pray. Amen.

As we part ways for now, remember that this journey is ongoing. Continue to seek God's guidance, embrace the lessons learned, and walk in faith. The tides of transformation will carry you to places beyond your wildest dreams, and with God by your side, there is nothing you cannot overcome.

ACKNOWLEDGEMENTS

First and foremost, I want to extend my heartfelt gratitude to my sons, Nicholas and Ryan. You both are the lights of my life and the reason I strive to be the best version of myself every day. Ryan, your curiosity and wisdom beyond your years inspire me constantly. Nicholas, your boundless energy and infectious joy remind me of the beauty and wonder in every moment. Thank you for your unconditional love and for teaching me more about life and love than I could ever have imagined.

To my parents, Carl, Tracy, Shana, and Tim, your unwavering support and love have been the foundation upon which I have built my life. Carl, your strength and resilience have been a guiding light for me. Tracy, your nurturing spirit and constant encouragement have given me the confidence to pursue my dreams. Shana, your wisdom and kindness have been a source of comfort and inspiration. Tim, your steadfast belief in me has been a pillar of strength. Thank you all for your sacrifices, for believing in me, and for always being there when I needed you the most.

I also want to extend my deepest gratitude to my friends, especially my best friends, who have been my chosen family. Your unwavering support, encouragement, and love have been instrumental in my journey. You have stood by me through thick and thin, offering a shoulder to cry on, a listening ear, and the kind of unwavering support that has kept me grounded. Your friendship has been a constant source of strength and joy in my life. I am blessed to have each of you in my corner, cheering me on and lifting me up.

Each of you has played a vital role in shaping who I am today. Your love and support have been the anchors in my life, helping me navigate the turbulent waters and celebrate the calm seas. I am profoundly grateful for your presence in my life, and I dedicate this book to you as a token of my deep appreciation and love.

RESOURCE LIST

Scripture References:

1. **Proverbs 3:6 (NIV):** "In all your ways acknowledge Him, and He shall direct your paths."

2. **Jeremiah 29:11 (NIV):** "For I know the plans I have for you," declares the Lord, "plans to prosper you and not to harm you, plans to give you hope and a future."

3. **Isaiah 43:2 (NIV):** "When you pass through the waters, I will be with you; and when you pass through the rivers, they will not sweep over you. When you walk through the fire, you will not be burned; the flames will not set you ablaze."

4. **Psalm 119:105 (NIV):** "Your word is a lamp for my feet, a light on my path."

5. **Ecclesiastes 4:9-10 (NIV):** "Two are better than one, because they have a good return for their labor: If either of them falls down, one can help the other up. But pity anyone who falls and has no one to help them up."

6. **Proverbs 17:17 (NIV):** "A friend loves at all times, and a brother is born for a time of adversity."

7. **Philippians 3:14 (NIV):** "I press on toward the goal to win the prize for which God has called me heavenward in Christ Jesus."

8. **Psalm 121:1-2 (NIV):** "I lift up my eyes to the mountains—where does my help come from? My help comes from the Lord, the Maker of heaven and earth."

9. **Hebrews 6:19 (NIV):** "We have this hope as an anchor for the soul, firm and secure. It enters the inner sanctuary behind the curtain."

10. **2 Corinthians 5:17 (NIV):** "Therefore, if anyone is in Christ, the new creation has come: The old has gone, the new is here!"

Books:

1. **"The Pursuit of Happyness"** by Chris Gardner: An inspiring story of perseverance and overcoming adversity.

2. **"Uninvited:** Living Loved When You Feel Less Than, Left Out, and Lonely" by Lysa TerKeurst: A book about overcoming feelings of rejection and finding love in God.

3. **"It's Not Supposed to Be This Way:** Finding Unexpected Strength When Disappointments Leave You Shattered" by Lysa TerKeurst: A book on finding strength and hope amidst life's unexpected challenges.

Songs:

1. **"Rolling Hills" by Jill Scott:** A powerful anthem about embracing one's true self and finding strength in adversity.

2. **"Let Go" by DeWayne Woods:** A song about surrendering to God and trusting His plan.

3. **"Mirror" by Lalah Hathaway:** A song about self-reflection and growth that has helped many through tough times.

Movies:

1. **"The Pursuit of Happyness":** A film about Chris Gardner's journey from homelessness to success, highlighting the importance of perseverance and faith.

2. **"The Wizard of Oz":** A classic film that parallels the journey of self-discovery and the importance of trusting in oneself.

3. **"Teen Wolf":** A film about a teenage boy who learns to embrace his true self despite the challenges and fears.

Personal Growth and Reflection:

1. **Journaling:** Regularly writing down your thoughts and reflections can help you process your experiences and track your growth.

2. **Meditation and Prayer:** Set aside time each day for meditation and prayer to strengthen your connection with God and find peace amidst life's storms.

3. **Therapy and Counseling:** Professional help can provide support and guidance in navigating personal challenges and promoting mental health.

Support Systems:

1. **Support Groups:** Join groups where you can share experiences and find encouragement from others facing similar challenges.

2. **Mentorship:** Seek mentors who can offer wisdom, support, and accountability as you navigate your journey.

3. **Community Involvement:** Engage in community activities and organizations that align with your values and support your personal growth.